An Overcomers' Journey
From the Effects of Abuse
Through
Scriptural Prayers

By Priscilla Coleman

An Overcomers' Journey From the Effects of Abuse Through Scriptural Prayers- Priscilla Coleman

All scripture quotations are from the King James Version of the Holy Bible. The author used brackets to indicate italic words.

Copyright © 2015 by Priscilla Coleman
Printed by CreateSpace, An Amazon.com Company
Kindle Version Available

ISBN-13: 978-1516980093
ISBN-10: 1516980093

PRINTED in the UNITED STATES OF AMERICA

This book is dedicated with great gratitude to my Heavenly Father.

"But thanks [be] to God, which giveth us the victory through our Lord Jesus Christ."
I Corinthians 15:57

"And they overcame him by the blood of the Lamb, and by the word of their testimony..."
Revelation 12:11

Table of Contents

Part One
History of Abuse

Peaceable Outcome
Protection
Hurricane Sandy
Health/Wellness
Answer to Health Challenge
Relational Prosperity
Opportunity to Develop

Life Today
Get Results
Resist Old Mindsets
Keep the Victory
Partaking of Food
Believing God for a House
Another Church
Conclusion

Part Three

A Scriptural Prayer

Self-help Scripture Topics Alphabetized

KCM Resources

Acknowledgments

Thanks to Kenneth and Gloria Copland. The word of God taught through your ministry has changed my life.

Thanks to James G and Genesis for providing professional editors for this book.

Preface

"That I may publish with the voice of thanksgiving, and tell of all thy wondrous works."
Psalm 26:7

My story is not an unusual one. I have met many Christians and Non-Christians who were abused sexually, psychologically, and physically by relatives, friends or spouse. Similar to my experience, self-proclaimed Christians have been the abuser. As I struggled to recover from the effects of abuse, I needed 911 support daily, and sometimes minute-by-minute help to choose to live.

The purpose of this book is to provide the resource I wish I had during my struggle. First, I tell my story so people will know they are not the only one to have suffered some of what I found to be shameful experiences. My testimony serves to shine the light in dark places (**II Peter 1:19**). Second, I want to provide real help: the word of God. **"For the word of God [is] quick, and powerful, and sharper than any twoedged sword, piercing even to the dividing asunder of soul and spirit...and [is] a discerner of the thoughts and intents of the heart." Hebrews 4:12**

This book is written in Three Parts.

Part One- This section will tell my story in the order of the abuse and measures used to overcome. First, in Chapters One and Two, I discuss the abuses in my childhood and marriage. I didn't write about every detail or the extent of all the abuses. The information shared is to provide an understanding of what occurred. Second, in Chapters Three through Five, I recount the effects these abuses had on my physical and mental health. Lastly, in Chapter Six, I explain my need to forgive in order to be in the position to receive healing and freedom from the past.

Part Two- This section is about my life after the abuse ended at age fifty. In Chapters Seven and Eight, I describe some of the deliverances and victories experienced through revelation knowledge of the word of God. In Chapters Nine and Ten, I discuss the impact Kenneth Copland Ministries (KCM) has had on my life. The word of God taught through KCM transformed me from victim to overcomer in Christ Jesus. I am currently a partner with KCM.

Part Three- This is the section where I share one of my scriptural prayer petitions in Chapter Eleven. I sign and date all of my petitions as a reference point as evidence when I believe I receive my request. The main focus of this section is Chapter Twelve that provides self-help, with thirty-six scripture topics. More than five hundred verses are written out for your convenience to create your own scriptural prayers. Blank pages in this book, are provided for this purpose. These topics and scriptures were selected specifically because they are the answers I found in the word of God that provided deliverance. Also included in this section are resources of KCM that I used and continue to use in my spiritual growth.

I pray that those who are struggling with the effects of abuse, and aren't sure where to start, can find real help in this book. For those who want to read my story, I tell it in narrative form. The purpose of the third section is for those who want to begin the process of renewing the mind with the word of God towards healing. It is important to read the scriptures out loud to yourself as **"...Faith [cometh] by hearing, and hearing by the word of God." Romans 10:17**

"Thank you, Heavenly Father, in the Name of Jesus for the people who read this book. Let them be delivered, healed and set free by Your word. In Jesus' Name, Amen."

"Now the Lord of peace himself give you (insert your name) peace always by all means. The Lord [be] with you all."
                    II Thessalonians 3:16

Part One

History of Abuse

Effects of Abuse

Leaving the Past Behind

History of Abuse

Chapter One

Childhood

"The thief cometh not, but for to steal, and to kill, and to destroy: I am come that they might have life, and that they might have [it] more abundantly."
John 10:10

I was born into a "religious" family that called themselves Christians, but some of them did not have Christ-like behavior. Mom and Dad were married in 1950. There were six children born from 1953-1963. Dad was the pastor of a church in the basement of our house, and Mom sang for the church services. Dad was a strong personality who dominated Mom and us with controlling and abusive behavior. He often imagined that someone was misbehaving and then he slapped us in the face or beat us with his belt. When I was four years old, I had a special place in the lower cabinet in the kitchen to hide from my dad. I was terrified of him to the point that I did not talk at home or at school (I started Kindergarten at four years old because of my birth month). Mom was afraid of him especially when he had one of his screaming and yelling episodes. Once while arguing with her, he put his fist through the wall! But she never said anything bad about Dad. She believed he had good reasons for doing the things he did.

Parents' Separation

When Dad decided to leave Mom, he took the three oldest kids, ages six, seven and eleven, out of school without Mom's knowledge. We went to live with Dad and his girlfriend and moved twice in a year's time. We attended two different elementary schools during our time with Dad. Mom did not know where we were for about a year. Because I did not talk, (I lived in a state of fear) at the second school, I was placed in Special Education classes and speech therapy classes. His girlfriend hand made plaid uniform skirts without a pattern for my sister and I. We had to wear them to school, even though it was not a uniform school.

Dad and his girlfriend left us alone on one occasion, for a long time at his apartment after there was a shooting in the neighborhood. He told us "I need to go away." He left his dog in the hall in front of the door and put coins in a piggy bank and told us to use it only if we needed something. His girlfriend came to check on us a couple of times. He returned to the apartment after several weeks of absence as though nothing had happened. He didn't tell us why he left or where he had been.

After a year he went back to live with Mom, and she was happy that they were together again. Within a few weeks Dad talked with us (i.e., the three oldest, ages seven, eight, and twelve). He told us that he was leaving and that he loved us. Dad bought some groceries... large cans of vegetables, peanut butter, government cheese and some other things. We had to inform Mom that Dad was gone again because he did not tell her himself. Mom was devastated. She took medication to be able to work and sleep. Every day she was hopeful that he was coming back to her.

The three youngest kids, ages two, three and four, had to go live with Mom's sister at my Grandfather's house because Mom could not care for them. Mom said her nerves were too bad to deal with kids. Mom and the three oldest kids moved to another house that was in disrepair. It had holes in the roof so the outside sky could be seen from inside. When it rained outside my bed got wet. There were large rats running throughout the house, and it was infested with roaches. Mom left for work at 5 a.m. We got ourselves up for school, (my now fourth elementary school) and prepared breakfast in the morning. One time when I toasted bread with margarine in the frying pan, the stove caught on fire (I was seven years old). The fire department came in with axes and left holes in the walls that Mom could not repair. Everyday when Mom came home from work she prepared dinner and went to her room because her nerves were too bad to deal with us. If we made noise she would ask us to be quiet. We tiptoed around the house when she was at home.

Mom did not know how to manage money and sometimes could not pay the bills. I used to pray that she would have money to pay the rent. One windy day when we were walking to school we saw money rolling down the street. We ran after it and caught the money. It was just enough for the rent for that month! Praise Jesus!

Living with Abusive Relative

We lived in the run-down house for about a year when Mom was unable to continue paying the rent for the house. She also had very little money for food so we had to go live at my Grandfather's house. That is where the three youngest kids were living with Mom's sister. The house was dark and dingy because Mom's sister didn't allow anyone to open the blinds and windows. Now all six children from the ages of three to thirteen years old were living together with Mom, her sister, her sister's husband and my Grandfather. Mom left for work at 5 a.m. and left her sister to care for us. Mom was still stressed out after the break up with my Dad and needed medication to work and to sleep. Mom's sister did not work and needed Mom's income to pay the mortgage and bills. Her husband was working a minimum-wage job. My Grandfather was retired and was sick. There were daily arguments between Mom and her sister because of her sister's controlling and violent behavior. Mom had grown up being dominated by her sister who even then said belittling and hurtful things so that Mom would be quiet and go to her room.

From the moment we moved to my Grandfather's house Mom's sister became in charge of Mom and us. It was as though Mom was no longer our mother because we had to get permission from her sister to do everything. We enrolled in another school; this was my fifth elementary school and I was eight years old.

In this book I shall call Mom's sister Trouble.

Trouble controlled every aspect of our lives...
money, food, when and if we went to school,
clothes, time, everything! Trouble even controlled
my Grandfather in his own house until he got sick
and left to live in a hospice setting. When Mom got
a paycheck she had to give the money to Trouble
to decide how it would be spent and she gave mom
an allowance. At mealtime Trouble decided who
ate and would not eat based on how well she
thought we followed instructions that day.

My bedroom was the smallest room in the
house, there were no windows and the walls were
painted a dark color. My room was a place of
punishment, as Trouble locked me in the room
many times. I had to call or holler out for Trouble
to get permission to leave my room to use the
bathroom. Many times I just held my urine and
stool so I would not get yelled at for disturbing her.
Trouble's daily conversation was abusive and
demeaning. Trouble said I was dumb and stupid
and would never be anything in life. Trouble told
me that I would not make it in this world because I
was ugly. She said maybe I could get a man to
marry me and take care of me, but that probably
wouldn't happen.

When one of the younger kids did something
Trouble didn't like, the older kids would get a
beating for not stopping them from misbehaving.
It was impossible for the older kids to know what
the younger kids were doing. We were not allowed
to be in the same room at the same time without
Trouble being present; we were told, "You might
act nasty with one another."

We were not allowed to go outside to play or have friends. Trouble told us she did not like being alone, therefore she couldn't allow us to attend school. Mom was not aware that we were not going to school until one of the school officials contacted her by phone at work. When Mom returned home she argued with Trouble about this. Mom told Trouble the authorities would come to the house if we did not go to school. Trouble still kept us out of school sometimes, but not months on end as before.

One time when my older brother was allowed to attend school, before returning to the house, he told a neighbor that Trouble was treating us badly. The neighbor, who was also a member of the church we attended, came over to ask what was going on. Trouble said that my brother was lying. The neighbor accepted that answer and walked away. Trouble said that we do not talk to anyone about our lives. All the oldest kids got a beating with the ironing cord that was made of twisted ropes with a strand of metal in it. This was to remind us that we should not talk to anyone if we were allowed to go to school. I had marks all over my body that bled and left scars.

Trouble stated that she was a Christian and if we didn't do everything her way, God would get us and we would go to Hell. She had Bible study at the house. Trouble used scriptures in a twisted way to say that we had to do everything we were told or we would die and go to Hell. We went to church sometimes and everyone in the church thought Trouble was wonderful for helping Mom with six children. We all went to church to get baptized and at the house Trouble had tarry service for us to receive the Holy Spirit, speaking in tongues. I was blessed to have received the Holy Spirit at age eight and I began to read my Bible believing someday God would save me from Trouble.

That same year, I got watery blisters all over my body. Trouble said I had a sexually transmitted disease. She said I had acted nasty with a boy when I was allowed to go to school. Even though I knew that was not true, I felt guilty and popped the blisters open to try to get rid of them. We did not have health insurance so I could not go to the doctor. During this time, on a hot day Trouble took all of us kids to her girl friend's house, which was a member of the church. We were not allowed to go inside. We had to sit outside in the sun on a bench and not move for hours. The sun popped some of the blisters open and I became very sick. Mom found a doctor who practiced medicine in his house and let her pay what she could. The doctor told Mom I had chickenpox and the blisters had become infected. I received a penicillin injection and medication the doctor had in his house.

Sexual Abuse

Trouble had a bedroom in the basement of the house and when I was nine years old, she sexually abused me for the first time. I lived in constant fear of being called to the basement and that fear took over other parts of my life. I continued to pray and read my Bible everyday crying out to God to save me from Trouble.

When I was ten years old I decided the only way out of the sexual abuse was to kill myself. I got a knife from the kitchen and went into the bathroom. I was not allowed to go to the bathroom without Trouble's permission. When Trouble realized that I was in the bathroom and not in my room, she repeatedly knocked and pushed on the door for me to come out. When I told Trouble that I was sick, she walked away. By God's grace I was not able to commit suicide. When my menstrual cycle began at age twelve, Trouble didn't sexually abuse me anymore.

Life of Lack

When I went to school I was often dirty and smelly because we did not have a washing machine or money for the Laundromat. The only way to wash clothes was on a washboard in the basement sink and hang them up on the clothesline in the basement. I did not want to go to the basement. I was also smelly because whenever I went to the bathroom to bathe Trouble would open the door and come in. I learned to wash up quickly in the sink and not take a bath. I didn't want to give Trouble the opportunity to sexually abuse me.

There were many times the utilities (water, electricity, and gas) were cut off because Mom couldn't afford to pay the bills. Mom was taking care of nine people on her one salary because the person with the minimum-wage job was unemployed many times. And Trouble refused to work.

When I went to school people called me names and picked on me because I smelled and the clothes I wore were hand-me-downs or from the used-clothes store. The clothes were worn-out looking and were either too big or too small. My shoes often had holes in them, and were either too big or too small. I got my first nice, new blouse, jumper and shoes <u>my size</u> when I was in junior high.

When I was in high school, Mom could no longer afford to pay the mortgage for the house she and Trouble had inherited from my Grandfather several years earlier. When they received a foreclosure notice in the mail, Mom didn't know what to do. I prayed, got the Yellow Pages and found a mortgage company that did second trust loans. I contacted the company for them and prayed over the paperwork as I completed it. Mom and Trouble agreed and signed the contract.

After a year Mom could not pay the first and second mortgage. The second company paid them a fraction of what the house was worth to move out of the house.

Trying to Break Free

When we left my Grandfather's house, Mom and Trouble got their own separate houses for rent. Trouble convinced Mom to move to a house near her. Even though we lived in separate houses, Mom still allowed Trouble to be involved in our lives. Trouble called the house several times a day to give her opinion about something or came to the house to be sure everyone was following her orders.

Two siblings had the courage to move and live on their own and go to college when Mom lost Grandfather's house. Trouble of course said bad things about them. Three of us moved with Mom, and my youngest sister continued to live with Trouble. The four oldest kids graduated from high school, and went to local colleges, two graduated from college. The two youngest kids didn't get past the eighth grade. Trouble kept them out of school most of their lives. They both said they would get a GED but never did.

Death of Youngest Brother

My youngest brother died at the age of twenty in a police incident. By this time we were living in a separate house from Trouble. Even though he lived with Mom Trouble was allowed to call everyday to harass him, with statements like "You are not saved, and are going to Hell." On the night my brother disappeared Trouble called to harass him. He immediately left the house, went out on his motorcycle and did not return to the house. He had been missing for a week, when Mom read in the newspaper that a body was found in our area. By the description of the body and clothes the person was wearing, Mom was sure it was my brother. My older sister and I called the phone number that was listed in the newspaper and went to a police station to make a positive identification from photographs. His body had been sent to Baltimore as John Doe.

The police said that he had drowned in a swimming pool about 20 minutes from our house. They said the police were chasing him for some reason when he got off his motorcycle and ran. They said he jumped the fence in the back yard of a house that had a swimming pool on the other side of the fence. We asked why the residents of the house or police did not call for emergency help for our brother (he could not swim). They responded that no one knew that he was in the swimming pool. They stated the officers lost him in the chase and didn't know where he was. They also stated that the residents of the house were not aware of any activity in their back yard until the next morning when they saw a body floating in their pool.

We were surprised when we saw prominent and multiple bruises in the photographs on our brother's forehead and bruises on the knuckles of both hands (he had a very dark complexion). His body also did not have any swelling or signs that he had been in water overnight. We asked about the bruises, and how they knew he had jumped the fence in the yard if they had lost him in the chase. The police refused to give a response. When we returned home, my sister and I told Mom that we believed there was more to the story than the police were saying. Mom's reply was, "Whatever happened between your brother and the police will not bring him back." She told us to not contact the police again about the matter. The coroner did not perform an autopsy. The death certificate noted the cause of death as drowning.

Mom called my Dad's sister to find out where he was, and he came to the funeral. Mom thought Dad had also come back to reunite with her. Mom believed this because Dad stated that he could not return to his girlfriend and therefore was homeless. After a few weeks Dad worked things out with his girlfriend and left. Dad was gone again, and Mom was grieving over it. One week after my brother's funeral I met the man I married (I discuss this in Chapter Two).

Death of Younger Sister

My younger sister lived with Trouble longer than of any of us, from two years old until she died at the age of twenty-four. My sister rarely talked and spent the least amount of time in school then all of us. When we were growing up, Trouble kept all of us in separate rooms so we had no interaction with one another apart from Trouble being present in the room. During my sister's life I only had a few conversations with her.

I was married when my sister was diagnosed with leukemia. I was afraid to see Trouble and did not visit my sister while she was hospitalized the first time. I drove to the hospital one night and stayed in my car in the parking lot almost all night praying for her. By God's grace she went into remission and was released from the hospital.

A few years later my sister became ill again, and Trouble refused to let her go back to the first hospital. Trouble told Mom and my sister that the hospital was trying to give her cancer. The second hospital where my sister was admitted had a reputation for providing subpar care. People we knew with minor ailments had died there. I begged Mom to take my sister back to the first hospital. But Mom listened to Trouble who insisted that my sister stay at the second hospital.

On the Friday before my sister died, I prayed and got the courage to visit her in the hospital. When I arrived Trouble followed me to my sister's room and said mean and hateful things to me. I did not respond to any of her comments and was praying in my mind.

Finally Trouble left the room, and I was able to talk with my sister. I told her that I had not visited because I did not want to see Trouble. I asked my sister to forgive me for not visiting and for not doing anything to make her life better. She forgave me and told me she understood. A doctor came in the room while I was there and talked with me about coming back the next week for a bone marrow match. I asked questions about the procedure and what the prognosis was for my sister.

Two days later, on a Sunday morning I called the hospital to check on my sister's condition. The nurse told me my sister died that morning. I asked to speak with the doctor on duty. I asked why the doctors had not requested a bone marrow match from our family early in my sister's treatment. I said that my sister would probably be alive had they done so. The doctor's reply was surprising. He said, "Your sister did not die from leukemia; the disease was not active; she died of complications from medications." I asked him to explain what that means and how this could happen. He did not give a reply.

I immediately called Mom and found out the hospital had not informed her of my sister's death. I told Mom what the doctor said about the cause of death. I wanted to find out what happened to my sister so this would not happen to another person. Mom's reply was, "Investigating what happened to your sister will not bring her back." Mom insisted that I not contact the hospital again. The death certificate noted the cause of death as sepsis not leukemia. My sister died six years after my brother died. Dad came back for her funeral. Mom once again thought he was back for good, but he stayed for a few weeks and then left.

Death of Father

At the age of sixty, six years after the youngest girl died, Mom got word from Dad's sister that he was dead. I do not know the circumstances that led to his death. I know he had been in the hospital multiple times for 30 days or more each visit, years earlier. The death certificate noted the causes of death as adenocarcinoma carcinoma and adenocarcinoma of the rectum.

Mom was devastated at the news of his death because she loved him very much and thought they would reunite. Dad was buried in New Orleans before his family was aware of his death. His girlfriend/wife wanted Dad's family to send her money to help raise their kids. Mom had a memorial service for him at the church.

Death of Mother

Three years after Dad died, at age sixty-eight Mom got sick, and fell out on the floor. My older sister came to visit Mom in the afternoon and Trouble was there. Mom had been on the floor since that morning, Trouble had not called an ambulance and didn't get her any medical help. My sister called an ambulance that took her to the hospital. When Mom arrived at the hospital she was in a coma. I wanted to visit, but was afraid to see Trouble. The next day, my sister called me on the phone and said Mom was not doing well, and the doctors could not find the cause of her illness. After a few days I decided to visit because I didn't want Mom to die without asking her to forgive me for the years I had not returned her calls, and been rude to her. I was very nervous and prayed as I went to the hospital. Trouble met me at the hospital door, and said something rude. I continued walking to Mom's room without responding. She did not follow me to the room.

My two oldest siblings were there when I arrived. Mom suddenly woke up and looked at us. I asked her to forgive me and she said that she would. Mom went back into a coma that evening. That weekend she went into cardiopulmonary arrest. Mom did not have a living will or advance directive. The hospital performed CPR for 45 minutes and put her on life-support equipment.

The hospital scheduled a meeting with us (two brothers, one sister and myself) in order to get written directions should Mom go into cardiopulmonary arrest again. The doctor informed us that all of her organs were failing and that she was dying. They gave us two options for her care. The first option was to stop all treatment and keep her comfortable with pain medication. The second option was to continue all treatment including life support. My siblings and I chose the second option. We added that if her heart stopped while on the machines they should not perform CPR. We prayed that the will of the Lord would be done.

The doctors wanted to know if we wanted to be called if she was near death, so that we could be present at her passing. My older sister and I wanted to be called. A few days later we got the call. We read scriptures and sang songs to her until she passed.

The cause of Mom's illness was discovered postmortem. The death certificate noted the cause of death as "Metastasis Carcinoma to Liver and Carcinoma Cervix" (sic). Mom died three weeks after she passed out on the floor. I was told by my older sister that a few years before Mom's death she had had a dilation and curettage. Trouble told Mom that the doctor was trying to give her cancer. Mom did not follow up with the doctor after the procedure and was afraid to seek any medical treatment after that.

Mom's life insurance policy was just enough to get a good funeral arrangements and burial spot. My older sister took care of the details. Mom was buried at the same cemetery as my Grandparents, younger brother and younger sister. The four of us kids and Trouble were Mom's beneficiaries. After the funeral costs were paid, each of us received $65.00. Trouble called my older sister to complain, asking, "Why did I get such a little bit of money?" My sister explained to her the cost of the funeral and burial. Trouble's response was "You should have paid less for all that." Trouble wanted more money and requested Mom's wedding rings. We didn't comply.

Trouble Don't Last Always

Four years after Mom died a relative called to say that Trouble was dead. I was told Trouble was in a diabetic coma for some time. After recovering from the coma her health was never the same. She was seventy years old when she passed. My older sister told me that it took one month to bury Trouble because her husband did not have an insurance policy or money. He begged charities and churches for money to have the funeral and burial. Her burial place is not with the family. I did not attend the funeral.

Chapter Two

Marriage

"…In the world ye shall have tribulation: but be of good cheer; I have overcome the world."
John 16:33

As stated in Chapter One, Dad came to my youngest brother's funeral. Mom wanted them to reconcile. I was still living with Mom at the time and was very angry with Dad. I went to church and out of frustration told a lady that I was going to marry the first man I met in order to get away from Mom and Dad. Here is an example of being careful what you say, because that is exactly what happened.

Dating

One week after my youngest brother's funeral I met a man at a church service who was ten years older than me and was divorced. He said he had grown up in the church and was a Christian. We went on our first date on my twenty-fourth birthday. A few months later, I told him about the abuses from my childhood. He told me he also had a troubled childhood but didn't share the details.

During the time we dated he periodically could not be contacted for several days. I decided to end the relationship because he was not dependable. I called him on the phone to tell him I didn't want to date anymore. He called me back later and said, "Thanks a lot. Because of you, I just had a car accident!" I felt guilty, thinking I somehow caused misfortune, so we continued to date. During the time we dated, he never told me he loved me. Whenever I asked if he loved me he always quoted this: "Love is the complete giving of oneself to an object of adoration; since I adore you, I love you."

After eight months of dating, he proposed marriage. I prayed, not asking God for His direction, but with the mindset that marriage was an opportunity for a better life. The response I received from God was "If this is what you want I will bless you in it." When I told Mom I was getting married she replied, "He is not like us." I didn't know what she meant and didn't ask. I got married eleven months after our first date.

In this book I shall call the man I married Tribulation. As we prepared for marriage, Tribulation found his wedding band at a friend's apartment. I bought my own wedding band at a discount store. My engagement ring was purchased at the department store where I worked. I purchased the ring with my own money and store discount. Then Tribulation paid the balance. These events were foreshadows of married life.

Psychological Abuse

When I met Tribulation I had been a victim of psychological abuse all my life. This abuse continued in married life. The National Coalition Against Domestic Violence (NCADV) www.ncadv.org, provide an in-depth definition of psychological abuse on their website. As I understand it, psychological abuse is present when one person uses control and power over another person to emotionally manipulate that person for self-centered interests. The manipulator creates a false sense of reality of what is appropriate and inappropriate at the expense of another to produce conformity. The manipulator demands obedience and compliance through multiple methods to maintain control and power. Some psychological abuse methods I experienced were:

- Blaming others
- Guilt trips
- Control over physical freedoms
- Isolation from others
- Outburst of anger/yelling
- Silent treatment/unavailable
- Upset the stability/function of life
- Lying/deception
- Threats of violence
- Withdrawal of affection
- Playing the victim (poor me)
- Withdrawing economic support

The Early Days

I married Tribulation during my third year in college. He controlled everything I did. For example, he instructed me to return to the apartment by a certain time after class or work, and I obeyed. He bought and selected my clothes. Tribulation said, "I own you, and you belong to me. If you leave me I will find you." He also told me that he had to treat me bad in order for me to know when he was treating me good.

The first week after marriage, Tribulation went to take the trash out and didn't come back until the next day. When he returned he said he had something to do but did not provide details. This became a pattern that increased to disappearing for several days at a time. I once called someone who he knew, to see if they had heard from him. Tribulation was very angry and told me to never do that again. He told me normal people go out like this, and I didn't know because I was out of touch with what "real" people do. I prayed for him to change; I blamed myself. I thought I was the reason he was not coming home and staying out for days on end.

Conceiving Children

I thought if we had children, Tribulation would have a nicer personality and would also come home everyday. He talked a lot about wanting children when we dated. After two years of not becoming pregnant, I finally went to the doctor. After a physical exam and answering medical and family history questions, the doctor said I would not be able to conceive. My mother had taken the medication diethylstilbestrol (DES) when she was pregnant with me to stop miscarriage. I was told, "Daughters of DES mothers are sterile." A second doctor gave the same diagnosis.

There was a night service at the church I attended, and a guest minister preached about Hannah. She was a woman in the Bible who could not conceive children, but prayed and conceived. After reading her story I prayed, and was prompted to take multivitamins and mediate on the story of Hannah.

With two more years passing by, I became very discouraged. On a Sunday morning, I decided enough was enough and to leave the marriage. Tribulation was not at the apartment when I packed some clothes in my car and went to church. I didn't know where I would live, but would stay in a hotel that night.

I became very sick while at church and had to return to the apartment. Tribulation was at the apartment when I returned and took me to urgent care. After the doctor did blood work, he said, "You will be fine in 9 months." I was excited, Tribulation told everyone in the waiting area that he was having a baby. I thought, now things are going to get better!

Disappearing Acts

Married life did not improve when I was pregnant. When I was six months pregnant, I tried to stop Tribulation from leaving the apartment. He grabbed my arm really hard and told me he was going out anyway. I understood then that I could not stop him from going out as he pleased.

When the child was born, Tribulation was there at the birth but did not return to the hospital until I was being discharged three days later. When questioned about this, his reply was, "I needed time to myself after dealing with you being pregnant." He dropped me off at the apartment and returned after several days.

While in labor with my second child, Tribulation had me wait saying he had something to do. He smelled like smoke when he returned to take me to the hospital. He took the older child to his mother's house and disappeared. After three days he came to drive me home from the hospital stating that I had gotten on his nerves, and he didn't want to see me; that's why he had not been to the hospital. Tribulation left after dropping me off at the house, and that day I drove myself to the store to buy baby formula.

House

After the first child was born I wanted to move out of the apartment into a house. At first Tribulation was supportive of the idea and even helped when there was a challenge to purchasing the house I selected. When we moved into the house he changed his mind about being a homeowner. He blamed me for removing him from the comfortable life he had living in an apartment. The house was built in 1949 and needed some work. I cut the grass, painted, stripped floors, etc. Every summer I selected a project to do in the house and enjoyed doing the work myself. Sometimes Tribulation helped with the projects.

After a few years in the house, Tribulation began to keep his paychecks and not help pay for the basic things for the family. He paid only the mortgage. I maxed out all of my credit cards to buy food, clothes for everyone (including Tribulation), car insurance for my car and his, the electric bill, gas bill, water bill, upkeep of the house, and the kids' activities, etc. Tribulation said that his friends told him because I was a younger woman, I was going to run off with a younger man, so he better take care of himself by keeping his money.

Secret Revealed

After five years of living in the house, Tribulation was arrested for Driving Under the Influence (DUI). It was then that I found out about his alternative life style and addiction to substances. I attended the arraignment hearing and was shocked when I saw him with red nail polish on his fingernails and toes, wearing my clothes, and women's shoes! When we got back to the house I told him I was leaving the marriage. His first response was, "Where are you going to go, you have nowhere to go." Then he responded, "You can't leave me. But if you do and take my children there is no place you can hide that I will not find you." I took this statement as a threat. The children were ages four and seven when this occurred. I remained in the marriage fourteen years after that conversation until the youngest child graduated from high school.

After his arrest, Tribulation openly practiced his secret lifestyle. He also put alcohol in the refrigerator, sat on the back porch to smoke marijuana and left sexual paraphernalia (rubber penis, breast with nipples, etc.) in the house and car. Almost every night when the children went to bed (their bedrooms were on the second floor of the house), he dressed up in women's clothes, make-up, nail polish, and wig and went out to transvestite clubs. I did not share a bedroom with Tribulation at this point. My bedroom was on the first floor by the front door of the house and he had a bedroom in the back of the house on the first floor.

When Tribulation went out there were times when he was so high on substances he lost his car keys at the club and called me (normally it was 2 a.m. to 4 a.m.) to bring his spare keys. I prayed that the children would be safe at home alone while I was gone. Normally I got a few hours of sleep but still got the kids up for school and went to work.

A few months after Tribulation's arrest, one of the children wanted to watch a video, and turned on the VCR that had a pornographic video of men and boy transvestites having sex. I stopped the video just before the child could see what was on the tape. I begged Tribulation to not bring his outside activity to the house because of the children. Tribulation told me to get a life. He said if I had a life I would know this is what normal people do. I was on constant guard to protect my children from drugs, alcohol and pornographic material.

Trying to Cope

I prayed, and prayed for Tribulation to change. I asked him to go to marriage counseling with me. He refused stating that he was his own therapist and there was nothing they could tell him. He said his lifestyle is what normal people do. He told me, "No one lives like you do. Reading the Bible and going to church is abnormal." I thought if I did what Tribulation wanted (pay all the bills, follow all his rules) things would be more peaceful at home, but that did not happen. Whatever I did was not good enough for him. He was verbally abusive and often stormed out of the house after talking with me, stating what I said or did was the reason he needed to leave the house.

I also did not have frequent interaction with my family in an effort to please him. Tribulation did not want me to interact with my family and always blocked the interaction. He didn't want his kids around some of them. Once when my older sister called the house Tribulation told her to never call his house again.

Dangerous Situations

Two years after Tribulation's arrest, I arrived home from work with my youngest child in the car, and a man was coming out of the basement window of the house. He walked straight to my driver's side window and said something, but I could not understand what he said. I was praying in my mind all the time; my heart was racing. He told me to put down my window, but I did not obey. I know it was God that told me to say to him through the glass, "Sir, I don't have anything to say to you." Then he walked off. I called the police who came with a police dog to check to the house to be sure no one else was inside. They asked me who else lived in the house. By that time my older child had come home on the school bus. I told him Tribulation lived at the house also. The police waited for him for a while then left.

I called Tribulation to tell him that someone had broken into the house. He asked me questions about what the police had done at the house and hung up the phone. I waited for Tribulation to come home for hours. I called him back but I didn't get an answer. Several days later he came home and went straight to the basement and I followed him. Tribulation became angry and told me to mind my business.

Time to Go

During the twenty-fourth year of marriage, I heard a man on the radio preach on the subject of the born again believer's responsibility of maintaining a holy environment in which we live for the Holy Spirit in us. I felt that message was for me. It became clear to me that I was not living within the will of God for my life. It was during this time I received a negative doctor's report. (I will discuss in detail the effects the marriage had on my physical and mental health in Chapter Five). I believed I needed to end the marriage for my health's sake.

I wished that Tribulation would leave the house and not return, then, I could end the marriage and keep the house. I wanted desperately to keep my house! As I prayed for wisdom and direction of what to do I was prompted to read the scripture:

"For what is a man profited, if he shall gain the whole world, and lose his own soul? or what shall a man give in exchange for his soul?"
Matthew 16:26

I said, "Lord, I love you more than this house, it is time to go."

During spring break of that year I began the process of leaving the marriage. I checked out a book from the library that discussed steps to take when leaving an abusive relationship. There were strategies listed of what to do before leaving the relationship. These steps did not alert the abuser and helped the victim be prepared and get out safely. The author suggested the victim and children have medical check ups, refill prescriptions, oral health check-ups, etc. He suggested making copies of important documents (house deed, marriage license, bills, IRS taxes from previous years). He also noted the importance of having original documents such as social security cards, health/life insurance documents, birth certificates, etc. He also suggested the victim open a separate checking account. I also decided to pay all bills to be sure they were current the months before I left.

The summer of 2008, as usual I began house projects. Tribulation knew that I always had a summer clean up/beautification project. Shredding old documents, giving away clothes and things was not unusual. That year I shredded over 20 years of documents. I gave away most of my clothes, coats, boots and shoes to charity organizations that helped the homeless. I didn't want the things to be sold, but given to those in need. It was important to me to give away things that were in excellent condition. Things that were worn out or undesirable, I put in the trash. I did not give away or take furniture items from the house when I left the marriage. It was important to me to leave everything but my personal belongings in the house. I wanted the children to be able to return to the house of their childhood without it looking stripped.

(**Side note**: It was amazing to me when I needed clothes as a child and furniture when I left

Tribulation that people thought I should be appreciative for worn out and undesirable left overs. One lady offered me a bed that her dog had urinated on. Another lady offered me undesirable furniture. When I told her didn't want it, she became offended. I believe that people should know that just because a person is in need doesn't mean they are less human and should appreciate inferior things).

Without Tribulation's knowledge, I applied for an apartment twenty-three miles away from the house. It was in a secure building with keyless entry into the garage and apartment complex. Due to Tribulation's previous threats, my priority was to move into a place where he could not easily gain access. The rent was more than the mortgage at the house. I couldn't see how I could afford to pay the rent, utilities, and credit cards and buy food, but thought I would be safe at this place. I sold my gold jewelry to have the down payment for the apartment. I also sold my wedding rings for the first month's rent. Tribulation was seldom at the house and paid such little attention to me when he was there, he didn't notice I wasn't wearing my wedding rings.

The summer of 2008 I left the house; my oldest child began her junior year at Towson University, and my youngest child began his freshman year at NYU. I moved them both into their dorms without help from Tribulation. When I returned from New York City, Tribulation was sitting on the back porch in full drag, legs crossed and smoking a large marijuana cigar. I waited for the perfect day and time to leave the marriage.

One month after I returned from New York, on a Sunday morning, three months before my fiftieth birthday, Tribulation said to me, "We are going to church." When I told him I was not going, he said, "I will go by myself." I was surprised that he did this, but recognized this as God providing an opening for me to leave. I had already signed my apartment lease agreeing to move in that Monday. When he left the house for the one-hour service, I packed as quickly as I could. I loaded clothes and important papers in my car, left the house and drove to the apartment complex. I stayed in my car praying for several hours. Then I decided to ask the rental office staff if I could move in that day. Praise Jesus they said I could.

Breaking Free

I moved into a bare apartment and lived that way for a month, and went to work every day. I slept on the floor with only a small blanket--no pillow-- and sat on the floor to eat what little food I had. I didn't even have money to buy toilet tissue (I borrowed a roll from the school and replaced it when I got money).

After a few days Tribulation called my cell phone, and said angrily, "You left me. Do you realize you left me?" Tribulation began calling my cell phone every hour 24 hours a day, leaving threatening messages. I listened to the messages so I could record as many of them as I could. One Sunday on my way home from church, I listened to a message. First he said, "I am tired of you, do you hear me?" Then he said, "I know where you are living." I was so afraid that I ran to the rental office to tell them Tribulation was not allowed to know which apartment was mine. I fell and hit my face on the concrete steps. My cheek swelled immediately. I went to the emergency room. The doctor said I had a concussion and should not work for a week.

One month after I left, Tribulation came to my job, and security escorted him off the property. A co-worker who saw Tribulation removed, asked me about the incident. I shared some information about the situation and told her I was in need of some basic things in order to continue to come to work. She gave me some money and told another co-worker that gave me a bed, a plastic dresser, dishes, towels, bed linen, cups, forks, spoons and knives and some money. God is good!

A few weeks later, Tribulation called my daughter on her cell phone and said, "Tell your mother to run; I know where she lives." She asked, "What are you going to do?" He replied, "I'm not going to be the one to do it." My daughter called me at work to relay her father's message. She was afraid for my safety and advised that I not return to my apartment, but find somewhere else to go.

When I heard the fear in my daughter's voice, I prayed for God to strengthen me to not be so afraid of Tribulation. I heard God say to me, "When you fell and hurt yourself at the apartment, it was because you were running out of fear. When you lived with Tribulation I didn't let him hurt you." I called my daughter back and asked her to give a message to her father from me, "You better run. I have not done anything to you. God will not let anyone hurt me." Tribulation asked my daughter who I had been talking to, and then threatened to hurt a person he believed was responsible for my new courage.

I contacted the police about the threats. The police said he had not done enough to be arrested or for me file a restraining order/peace order. Their advice was to change my travel routines and the times I left and returned home each day. They told me that because he was an ex-police officer, he knew how to walk the line of threatening me but not doing enough to be arrested.

I originally intended to legally separate, not divorce Tribulation because the church I attended said divorce was wrong. Tribulation went to the church to inform them that I had left the marriage. He gave leaders of the church my cell phone number. They called me to remind me of church doctrine that a wife does not leave a marriage for any reason. One lady left a message on my phone stating that Tribulation was crying at church and was suffering.

Then I decided to divorce Tribulation. I went to free consultations with lawyers to file for a limited divorce. One lawyer told me to pay all the bills I had paid before I left Tribulation and that would stop him from harassing me. He said being a transvestite, homosexual/bisexual is accepted in society and substance abuse is an illness. The lawyer said I would have to pay spousal support because I left the marriage. He went on to say, Tribulation probably would get alimony and my pension. Another lawyer wanted $3,000 for his services and I did not have the money. More details about the divorce are in Chapter Seven. The divorce was final when I was fifty-one years old.

In the next section I will address the effects of the abuse of my past. According to the organizations NCADV (sited in the beginning of this chapter) and Adults Surviving Child Abuse www.asca.org, systematic long-term abuse causes mental and physical effects in the victim. Some of the effects they list are what I experienced:

- Depression/Suicidal thoughts
- Poor Health/Sickness
- Difficulty Sleeping
- Eating Disorders
- Panic Attacks
- Fear/Anxiety
- Post Traumatic Stress Disorder

The Effects of Abuse

Chapter Three

Fear

"For God hath not given us the spirit of fear; but of power, and of love, and of a sound mind."
II Timothy 1:7

The first effect of the abusive life was fear. I was afraid of Dad, Trouble, Tribulation, and that created a culture of fear in my mind about everything. I was afraid of dogs, afraid to walk outside alone, afraid to talk to people. I had feelings of terror and helplessness... the list goes on and on.

Childhood fears

Trouble allowed me to attend school more regularly by the time I was in the seventh grade. I was very afraid to walk to school alone. My older sister who was attending the same school had friends who walked with her, but they would not allow me walk with them. I followed them as closely as allowed. When there was a dog nearby, I became paralyzed with fear. My sister and her friends laughed and taunted me because I was afraid. I was afraid to go back home and afraid to move forward. But God always had someone walking down the street stop to help me get past the dogs. Thank you, Lord!

When I was promoted to the ninth grade, I didn't want to attend the local high school where my older sister and her friends attended. The chorus teacher at my junior high school told me about a new public performing arts school opening. It was called Duke Ellington School of the Arts. She said, "You have a beautiful voice." It was the first positive thing anyone had ever said to me. I didn't believe I had a beautiful voice, but was afraid to attend the local high school with the bullies. I wanted to audition for the new school to see if I would be accepted.

I had to get permission from Mom and Trouble to audition. The argument regarding this decision lasted for days because Mom thought I should audition but Trouble did not. This was the first time Mom stood up to Trouble. I was allowed to audition, and was accepted at the school. I often wondered how I would get to school across town because of the fear of being outside and of dogs. Also, I didn't know how I would get money for transportation. My younger brother, who was not attending school, volunteered to walk me to the bus stop every morning and wait for me at the bus stop every afternoon. God provided transportation through bus tokens. Trouble tried to make it difficult for me. She did not allow me to have a key to the house. One time when my brother came to meet me at the bus stop in the afternoon, Trouble left the house, locked the door and did not come back for hours. I broke a window to get into the house because I had to go to the bathroom.

Trouble beat me with a belt when she got home for breaking the window.

The beating did not have the same effect on me as the others had. I wore clothes that covered the marks on my body. It did not stop me from attending the school. People at Ellington treated me with kindness and thought I was talented. It was here I had my first friend, Carolyn. I increased my prayer life and read other scriptures on not being afraid. I quoted this and other scriptures to myself over and over speaking them out loud.

"The LORD [is] my light and my salvation; whom shall I fear? the LORD [is] the strength of my life; of whom shall I be afraid?"
Psalm 27:1

College fears

As my high school career was coming to an end, I began to fear what I was to do next in life. I was starting to believe that I had a talent for singing, but was unsure what to do. Other students applied to colleges, and the music departments had recruiters attend their senior recitals. Many of those students were offered scholarships on the spot. I didn't think a college recruiter would attend my recital because I had not applied to any colleges. To my surprise, a representative from Norfolk State University attended my recital. He was at Ellington that morning to hear another student, but stayed on through the afternoon to hear me sing. He offered me a full music scholarship (with room and board) including a stipend to sing in the university chapel choir. I asked Trouble and Mom if I could attend the college. Trouble and Mom were united in their decision; I was not allowed to accept the scholarship.

After high school graduation, I was afraid to apply to a four-year college fearing that I was not smart enough to attend and knowing I did not have the money for tuition. I was able to get a Pell Grant to attend a local community college one semester and then worked for three years at a department store. At age twenty-one, I saw a boy who was a high school classmate. He asked where I was attending college. I told him I was not enrolled in any college, but worked as a fitting room clerk and salesperson at a department store. He advised me to complete an application to Howard University. He told me the voice teacher from Duke Ellington, was a member of the music faculty there and would help me. I decided to follow the classmate's advice.

At this point in life Trouble was not living with us, but Mom still allowed her to be involved in the discussion of whether I could apply to Howard University. Mom decided against Trouble and allowed me to complete the college application. I applied, auditioned and was accepted into the music department. It was the spring semester and all the scholarships had been given out the previous fall semester. A college professor told me if I could get a student loan to start in January and audition for the entire voice faculty, I had a good chance of getting a scholarship in the coming fall. I prayed and read scriptures to overcome fear:

"Hear, O LORD, and have mercy upon me: LORD, be thou my helper."
Psalm 30:10

Mom knew nothing about getting a student loan so I had to do this all myself with God's help. I was very nervous when I went to the bank to ask someone to help me. By God's grace there was a man who was kind enough to explain the process and help me complete the loan application. My request was approved. During the spring semester, I auditioned for the entire voice faculty and received a four-year full tuition and fees scholarship. I continued to work at the department store part-time after classes and had a two-hour commute one-way to college. My younger brother continued to assist me because of my fear of dogs. He walked me to the bus stop at 6 a.m. and waited in the dark at the bus stop for my return in the evening.

My fear of not being smart enough for college often arose as I struggled in Freshman English class. In order to improve my reading and comprehension skills I created journals to use during my Bible study time. I wrote down words with the definitions of which I was not familiar. Each journal had the words listed alphabetically. When I came across the word again I could look it up in my journal. I also used my journals to learn how write in cursive. The Bible has some words written out phonetically and I wrote them exactly as they appeared in order to lean how to pronounce them. The dictionary, thesaurus and

Bible concordance provided a wealth of knowledge in my development.

Fear of driving

After my first year in college a distant cousin (who was a deacon at my church) pulled me to the side. He told me he noticed how hard I was working to attend college and helping Mom by working at the department store. He explained it would make my life easier if I had a car, and sold me a ten-year-old vehicle for $1.00. At the time, I did not know how to drive, and never had a driving lesson, nor could I afford them. When I first got the car, my older sister would use the vehicle. She didn't take the time to teach me to drive, but taught me how to park. After getting my learner's permit, I practiced driving with Mom as she had a driver's license. I learned to drive by taking her to the subway station every morning at 5 a.m. Mom was more fearful than I was about my driving but she had no other way to get to the subway (Mom always said she was too nervous to drive). I used scriptures to overcome the fear of driving. One example is:

"...Be strong and of a good courage; be not afraid, neither be thou dismayed: for the LORD thy God [is] with thee whithersoever thou goest."
Joshua 1:9

Even though I was shaking with fear, I drove anyway. For protection, I put one Bible in the back window and another on my lap. The best way I figured to drive the car would be to maneuver as though parking: stay between the lines. I would say this prayer every time I got behind the wheel of the car:

"Lord, go before me as a leading lamb and come behind me as a protective angel. Don't let me run into anybody, and don't let anybody run into me. Preserve the battery, brakes, tires and every part of the car. In Jesus' Name, Amen."

By God's grace I was able to pass the driving test within a few months. That car was a blessing to Mom and me, even though it needed several repairs. The car battery often needed a cola poured on it for a jump-start. Whenever it rained outside, water would leak inside the car on my foot. The headlights didn't light the road but shined up in the trees. The tires were almost bald. We didn't have money for repairs, just money to buy gas to get where we were going. God always took care of us. One day while I was driving a tire went flat. By God's grace a man stopped to help and gave me a tire from his car and changed the tire.

Flashbacks in Dreams
During this time feelings of terror engulfed me through dreams of the basement on Delafield Place where the sexual abuse took place. I also had a fear of the numbers 623, which was the house address. I often felt sick when the time of day was 6:23 or the date was June 23. I thought something bad was going to happen during those moments or time. I prayed for deliverance from the recurring

nightmares and the fear of the numbers. An example of a scripture often prayed was:

"...The former troubles are forgotten..."
Isaiah 65:16

There were times that I woke up from a nightmare quoting scriptures out loud or praying in the Spirit. I prayed for God to heal me completely from the memories and fears. After several years of praying, one day, I had a dream of the house looking brand new. Everything inside and out was bright and full of light. After that I didn't have any more nightmares about that house. I also didn't fear the numbers 623, the time 6:23 or the date June 23 anymore.

"When the LORD turned again the captivity of Zion, we were like them that dream. Then was our mouth filled with laughter, and our tongue with singing...The LORD hath done great things for us; [whereof] we are glad."
Psalm 126:1-3

Shame

The effects of the sexual abuse produced feelings of shame about my body. I wore long sleeves and turtleneck shirts all the time (even during Summer months) and dressed to cover my body completely. I prayed scriptures to be healed from shame:

"I sought the LORD, and he heard me, and delivered me from all my fears. They looked unto

him, and were lightened: and their faces were not ashamed."

Psalm 34:4-5

I even had a fear of being naked when cleansing myself. I could wash up with my clothes on but believed that something bad would happen to me if I took off all my clothes at one time. I spoke with another victim of sexual abuse who had the same problem. Once, I heard a preacher speak the following on the subject of shame:
"Before the fall of man in the Garden of Eden there was no shame present.

"And they were both naked, the man and his wife, and were not ashamed."

Genesis 2:25

"...But all things [are] naked and opened unto the eyes of him with whom we have to do."

Hebrews 4:13

When Jesus was scourged and crucified there was an exchange of our sin and shame that He took to give us His righteousness. The definition of righteousness is being right with God to receive all of His goodness, grace and mercy. Righteousness is ours because of the blood of Jesus sacrifice and His resurrection, not by our behavior or good works. It is all based on what Jesus did."

"For he (God) hath made him (Jesus) [to be] sin for us, who (Jesus) knew no sin; that we might be made the righteousness of God in him."

II Corinthians 5:21

I took courage in the preacher's message believing that God would help me. From my new discovery, I was prompted to begin a process to be free from shame of my body. I anointed myself with blessed oil (prayed over olive oil) the first day of the process, and washed myself wearing an elbow length blouse. As time passed, I removed more clothing, as I was able. After a year of doing this I was able to take off all my clothes and take a bath! Praise Jesus!

Panic Attacks

I began having anxiety attacks after being married for five years. By year ten of the marriage full blown panic attacks emerged. I worried constantly about everything, as there seemed to be no way out of daily problems. Tribulation was having his cake and eating it too. I was taking care of the real life issues, while he came and went as he pleased enjoying his life.

When I had a panic attack, I had extreme feelings of horror and I could not stop my body from rocking. During these periods I needed to be in constant motion. Often I walked around the house in quick rapid motion to try to get relief! For several months there was no escape from the panic attacks. I sometimes had two a day and developed a fear of the panic attacks!

I created a journal of my thought patterns and schedule in order to find a cause for the panic attacks. I found the main triggers were lack of sleep, lack of food, loud noise and worry. Scripture

instructs me to cast my care on God and receive
His peace:

"Be careful (anxious) for nothing; but in every thing by prayer and supplication with thanksgiving let your request be made known unto God. And the peace of God, which passeth all understanding, shall keep your hearts and minds through Christ Jesus."

Philippians 4:6-7

Praying this scripture and others everyday brought deliverance from the panic attacks, Praise Jesus.

Over time, I learned to identify the symptoms of an onset of an attack and was able to head them off. I focused on scriptures that were about giving God thanks and speaking of the victory through Jesus. I often sang songs of praise. One of my favorite songs to sing is "In the Name of Jesus." The lyrics to the song are:

Verse

In the Name of Jesus, In the Name of Jesus, we have the victory. In the name of Jesus, Precious name of Jesus, Satan will have to flee!
Tell me who can stand before us when we call on His great name, Hallelujah! Jesus, Jesus, Precious Jesus, We have the victory!

Chorus

Oh, Oh, Oh, Victory, Hallelujah, Victory!
We have the Victory!

Thank you Jesus!
Victory, Glory, Glory, Victory!
We have the Victory!

Chapter Four

Eating Disorder

"For no man ever yet hated his own flesh; but nourisheth and cherisheth it, even as the Lord the church."
Ephesians 5:29

A therapist once told me, "Hunger or the desire to eat is equivalent to the desire to live. It is a natural instinct that is present in a healthy human being." The National Eating Disorder Association (NEDA), www.nationaleatingdisorders.org, says, "Poor appetite and eating disorders can be the effect of physical, psychological and sexual abuse."

Early Experiences with Food
I believe abuse and early childhood experiences with food can shape eating patterns later in life. When I lived with Dad mealtime was a time of contention. He always cooked more food than could be consumed by a young child. When I didn't eat all the food on my plate he yelled and screamed. When I was four years old, during a yelling episode he said to me, "I don't like what you are thinking." He slapped me in the face, and my ears rang. The imprint of his hand stayed on my face for a week. I dreaded mealtime because it normally ended with some type of punishment.

Food Withheld

When I lived with Trouble food was withheld as a form of punishment. Everyday she decided who would and would not eat. I didn't expect to be selected to eat and didn't feel hungry when not chosen. When Trouble sexually abused me, I thought it was my fault because my body was developed at an early age. I withheld food from myself many days so I could lose weigh in hope of ending the abuse.

No Desire to Eat

I cannot remember ever feeling hunger or hunger pains. I could go days without eating food until I suddenly felt physically weak or sick and then I would eat. I realized later in life that I had such self-hate that it manifested in trying to kill myself by not eating.

After being married for seven years, I had symptoms of severe abdominal pain and uncontrolled vomiting episodes. My doctor was searching for a diagnosis and ordered test. When preparing for a CT scan drinking a white solution was required to get a good result. When I had trouble drinking the solution, the doctor told me to imagine it as my favorite food. I told the doctor I didn't have a favorite food. He began to name foods to help me with my imagination. I replied negatively to all the foods he mentioned. The doctor asked, "What do you eat?" I replied, "I eat when I have to, whatever is there, it really does not matter." He told me not having a favorite food and not enjoying food was abnormal.

After that, I noticed that other people had favorite foods and spent time talking about food. I then realized what the doctor said was true. I also realized not having a desire to eat and never feeling hunger was abnormal. I searched the library for books to help me overcome this problem. I thought surely I could not have been the only person with this problem. Unfortunately, I didn't find any information. I prayed for a solution and searched for all the scriptures I could find about eating. One of the scriptures I found is:

"And also that every man should eat and drink, and enjoy the good of all his labour, it [is] the gift of God."
Ecclesiastes 3:13

I was not aware that I was to enjoy things in life, such as food. The word "enjoy" was foreign to me. I tried unsuccessfully to apply the scriptures. I simply would forget to eat, because I really never felt hungry and had no desire to eat.

Prayers to Encourage Eating
I began a journal to write down my meals and the time of day that I ate. My goal was to eat something every two hours. I prayed for guidance and prayed this prayer every time I ate:

"Thank you God for something to eat, the time to eat, the mind to eat and the desire to eat. Please don't let the food make me sick, let it be only nourishing and strengthening to my body. In Jesus' Name, Amen."

I checked out cookbooks with pictures from the library to encourage me to think about food and to create a desire to eat. Watching cooking programs on television helped me see food differently and sometimes encouraged me to eat.

Later I realized God is never going to over ride my will. When I ask Him for help He answers, but He will only help when I ask. When I had no desire to eat, God was not going to push food down my throat. I had to want to eat, for Him to be able to help me. In Chapter Ten, I discuss partaking of food today.

"I [am] the LORD thy God...open thy mouth wide, and I will fill it."
Psalm 81:10

Chapter Five

Sickness

"Who his own self bare our sins in his own body on the tree, that we, being dead to sins, should live unto righteousness: by whose stripes ye were healed."
I Peter 2:24

The abuse of my past created chronic stress and was inescapable. The effects of stress manifested into sicknesses that took on different forms over the years as mental and physical illness. In this section the sicknesses discussed developed while I was married with exception of depression. The American Psychological Association's (APA) research found stress to be dangerous when it interferes with the ability to live a normal life. The longer the stress lasts, the worse it is for both the mind and body. On their website www.apa.org/topics/stress/index.aspx they state, "Chronic stress can damage a person's physical and mental health and may cause disease such as depression, gastrointestinal problems and other ailments."

GERD
Year seven of the marriage, I developed symptoms of severe abdominal pain, burning in my chest and vomiting after every meal. I was diagnosed with Gastro esophageal Reflux Disease (GERD). After an upper endoscopy the doctor

diagnosed Schatzhis ring, abnormal mucosa in the antrum and pylorus, Grade I Esophagitis and Gastritis as a causes for GERD. After being prescribed Proton Pump Inhibitors (PPI) the vomiting episodes ended. In addition to the PPI, I was prescribed a regiment of two antibiotics, and a host of other medications. This treatment was difficult to tolerate due to nausea as a main side effect.

Dietary Restrictions
APA's research found stress to be an indicator in gastrointestinal distress that can cause intolerance of certain foods. The year GERD was diagnosed; I began a restricted diet that was my plight for more then twenty years. The use of scriptural prayers and a journal to document what and when I ate, the Holy Spirit revealed the foods that kept my stomach calm. I ate most foods as long as they did not have seasoning or condiments on them. I seasoned foods with fresh celery, carrots and mushrooms, and bake and broil meats.

Foods Avoided:
Onions
Garlic
Citrus fruits
Tomatoes/ tomato sauces
Cinnamon
Peppermint
Pepper
All spices
All condiments
Excessive salt

Sea Salt
Whole milk
Chocolate
Coffee
Tea

Depression

    I had lived in a state of depression for as long as I can remember. There were levels to the severity. As a child I remember always feeling sad and like something bad was going to happen all of the time. I often felt a mental state of confusion and was totally unsure of myself about everything. I often cried myself to sleep at night. All my life I had believed I was born to suffer. I often thought if something good happened to me it was because I was getting ready to die. My life was often like a comedy of errors, one bad thing happening after another. My mindset was of self- hatred, I hated the way I looked, and had an inferiority complex. I also thought everyone deserved better things then I did. As I got older I developed a life style of not thinking. I didn't expect anything good to happen to me. I didn't have any goals, or dreams. I went with the day happening to me.

    During year fifteen of the marriage, I had a mental breakdown with severe depression and fatigue. I could not work and was blessed to have Sick leave bank so I could receive a paycheck. The doctor diagnosed Post Traumatic Stress Disorder (PTSD) and depression. She had to prescribe medication after medication, as I could not ingest them without vomiting it all back up. I was not able to take any medication. I had many suicidal thoughts. The mental pain and suffering was indecribeable! It felt as though just a turn of my head would cause my brain to fall out and I would die. I sat on the bed and held my head as still as I could from morning to night. It is only by God's grace that I did not kill myself. I began saying scriptures to myself over and over out loud to drown out the voice in my head that repeated over and over, "Kill yourself." The doctor told me since medication could not be tolerated I had to get well the slow way, through exercise, meditation and psychotherapy.

There were days that all I could do was cry all day and couldn't get out of the bed. One day when I got on my knees to pray crying out loud for God to help me, Tribulation yelled at me, "Shut up that noise." He was angry because I was too ill to care for the kids. Now he had to come home from work and stop going to clubs at night to be available for the kids. I also needed him to drive me to the doctor. While at the doctor's office, Tribulation was rude and argued with the doctor. He told her she'd better do something so I could get well. Whenever I was well enough to get out of bed, I went to psychotherapy, exercise class and to a prayer service held at the church during the day. I always made the bed, thanked God and prayed:

"Please help me be well enough to say out of bed, get something to eat, take care of my children and only get back in bed at night time." I would also pray the scripture:

"The LORD will strengthen him upon the bed of languishing: thou wilt make all his bed in his sickness."
Psalm 41:3

The therapist who was treating me said my married life was like the oppression from my childhood and this was causing the depression and PTSD. By God's grace I was able to return to work after ten months but continued to go to therapy sessions and exercise class when I could after work.

By year twenty-two year of the marriage, the symptom of severe depression emerged again, this time with chronic pain. I also was extreme tired all the time and I developed uncontrolled vaginal bleeding. The bleeding lasted for several months; but thank God I could use the Sick leave bank again, in order to receive a paycheck. The doctor's diagnosis was PTSD, large fibroids, severe anemia iron count at level 8 (the normal range is 35-155); the blood reserve was <1 (the normal range is 10-291). I was given an iron infusion and iron supplements and was monitored by a Hematologist for several weeks. Surgery was performed on my forty-eighth birthday to stop the bleeding source. I maintained psychotherapy but with a different therapist who strongly suggested to leave Tribulation for my health's sake. I told the therapist that I was afraid to leave. Praying the following scripture often caused the depressed mindset to began to lift:

"Lift up your heads, O ye gates; and be ye lift up, ye everlasting doors; and the King of glory shall come in."
Psalm 24:7

IBS

During year twenty-three of the marriage, I developed symptoms of Irritable Bowel Syndrome (IBS). The physician prescribed medication that I was not able to tolerate due to the side effects of nausea and vomiting. While in psychotherapy, I was told stress, fear, lack of sleep, worry, and skipping meals were causing the IBS symptoms. All of the causes of the IBS symptoms seemed impossible to avoid especially getting a good night's sleep.

Tribulation's nighttime routines were very disruptive to my sleep patterns. He went in and out of the house several hours throughout the night, opening and closing the garage door (my room was over the garage). Most times he drove off in his car, only to return moments later. He would do this all through the night. All of this activity made it impossible for me to sleep. There were many times he left the doors unlocked and I worried that someone would come into the house. I normally checked the doors throughout the night to be sure they were locked. I was very concerned for my children's and my safety.

The therapist said if I could sleep, it would give me a chance of correcting the other issues that were contributing to the IBS symptoms. She explained that lack of sleep affects the overall mental and physical health of a person. Therefore fear, worry and poor diet would continue to be challenges without sleep. I prayed this prayer:

"I will both lay me down in peace, and sleep: for thou, LORD, only makest me dwell in safety."
Psalm 4:8

Praying this, helped release my concern for safety to God, trusting that He would take care of the children and I. It wasn't immediate that I slept, but in time I could sleep at least five hours a night. Some mornings when I got up, the doors were unlocked, but God had kept us safe. Praise Jesus!

Prescription

I learned to seek God's wisdom for guidance when symptoms of sickness attack my body (**Proverbs 4:7**). In the early years of sickness I immediately became fearful when a diagnosis was discussed and did what ever the doctor advised. I now realize that doctors are "practicing medicine" and bring their personality, work ethic or lack of it to the profession. Seeking the wisdom of God for the right doctor and course of action is important. When I was diagnosed with other illnesses not shared in this book, I learned not to react immediately to the doctor's diagnosis, but tell the doctor I will pray about your findings and get back to you. Sometimes I took medication or had surgical procedures. Other times the wisdom of God was to wait, pray only, or try a natural method. Whenever I pray for the wisdom of God for a solution of a symptom, and get peace about the course of action, it always brings about healing.

Leaving the Past Behind

Chapter Six

Forgive

"And when you stand praying, forgive, if you have ought against any: that your Father also which is in heaven may forgive you your trespasses."
Mark 11:25

Some of the people who hurt me throughout my life were not apologetic and often found ways to hurt me more. I had a lot of hate and resentment towards them. I knew what the Bible said about forgiving others but somehow felt I was exempt from forgiving them because of what was done to me. In the process of leaving the past behind I learned that I needed to forgive the people that hurt me for my own sake. In the Mayo Clinic article, "Forgiveness: Letting go of the grudges and bitterness": November 11, 2014, medical professionals made the connection between holding grudges and illness. For the Christian, forgiveness is not a feeling but a decision to obey Jesus, then ask and expect the Holy Spirit to provide healing.

Mother

Mom was unavailable and unresponsive to the abuse that occurred at the hands of her sister. I thought Mom was a weak person and I resented her for that. When we moved from my Grandfather's house to our own house, I tried on several occasions to tell Mom what Trouble had done to me. Mom would say, "I don't know why you want to say things about Trouble, she was only trying to help you." Or she would say, "I don't want to talk about it, be quiet we don't discuss things like that." I asked Mom why we had lived with Trouble, why didn't she take care of us herself? Mom said, "If we didn't live with Trouble I would have had to put all of you in foster care or up for adoption, is that what you wanted? You should be thankful you kids didn't have to live in foster care or were adopted."

During the time of my marriage, Mom called asking me to transport my younger sister to the hospital as she had been throwing up blood for a month. My sister was still living with Trouble. Mom defended Trouble saying that she didn't have the time to take my sister to the hospital. My response was "You have never been a Mother to me or my other siblings. Your youngest child is dying, and I'm not coming!" Trouble eventually took my sister to the hospital.

I had a strong dislike for my Mother. Whenever it was Mother's Day or her birthday I searched for generic cards without the words "I love you" because those were not feelings I had at the time. As I continued to read my Bible everyday, it became clear forgiveness is not an option. I learned that forgiveness is a command from God. All that is required is a quality decision to forgive. I forgave Mother before she died.

Trouble

My mother's sister, Trouble continued to be abusive to my sister that lived with her. I thought surely, I was not to forgive Trouble because she had not changed. God dealt with my heart in this matter, and I knew I had to forgive her. My question to the Lord was, "Am I suppose to be around this person, take my children around her when I forgive?" The answer was in the scripture:

".... Because they have no changes, therefore they fear not God."
Psalm 55:19

I concluded that forgiveness is a matter of the heart not physical interaction with a predator. It was clear that if I interacted with Mom's sister, my children would be her next victims. One day at church, I walked over to her and said, "I forgive you for what you did to me." Her response was "I have not done anything to you." She reached her hand out to touch my daughter. I replied, "I have forgiven you so I can go on with my life. Don't you ever touch, talk or try to contact me or my children." I wasn't sure if that was a correct response, but wanted it to be clear.

Father

The time I lived with Dad was difficult, but not as bad as when I lived with Mom's sister. I blamed him for leaving me to suffer, and for taking advantage of Mom by calling over the years to ask for money. Mom always sent him money even when we didn't have food! I was very angry and told him so when he called me on the phone later when I was married. He tried to explain his situation, stating that Mom's controlling sister and family had driven him away. He said, "All I needed was for your mother to choose me over her family by letting me make decisions without their input and then I would have stayed." I didn't want to hear it, I just said every mean thing to him I could think of. He was very drunk when he called and was crying a lot.

A few years after the phone call, Dad sent me a post card from New Orleans. He wrote scriptures and statements about love. He wrote that the "God of peace is Love." Dad also wrote that he wished me happiness in marriage. After Dad died, I realized that he was a victim of Trouble in that she had stolen his family from him. From what I know about Trouble, Dad's integrity and manhood were challenged. It must have been difficult for Dad during the time Mom was letting Trouble control his life. I didn't forgive him before he died but I read:

"Whose soever sins ye remit (forgive) they are remitted..."
John 20:23

I took this scripture to mean that even though I didn't forgive Dad when he was alive, God would honor the fact that I had forgiven him. It would have been good to do it before he died, but forgiveness is my part not the other person.

Older Sister

As stated in Chapter Three, my sister often bullied me growing up. Two years after Dad died, my sister became very ill and was hospitalized for several weeks. It took several months to find a cause for her symptoms. One year after Mom died, my sister returned to the hospital and was near death. She refused to take life-sustaining medication on a regular basis and was waiting to die. I visited her in the hospital and told her, "You will live and not die, now take the medicine!" She apologized for being mean to me over the years. She had a hard time accepting that I cared if she lived or died. I accepted her apology.

During her hospital stay, I went to my sister's apartment rental office and paid her back and current rent, bought food to the hospital to be sure she ate and assisted with her medication until she was discharged. I cared enough to help her, but still had hard feeling toward her. Then, God dealt with my heart and told me I needed to forgive her. I found this scripture and obeyed:

"So that contrariwise ye [ought] rather to forgive [him], and comfort [him], lest perhaps such a one should be swallowed up with overmuch sorrow."
II Corinthians 2:7

Tribulation

In hindsight when dating Tribulation after sharing with him my abusive past, I should have asked him to share the details about his past. I wondered why Tribulation married me knowing his lifestyle and knowing that I was a naïve church girl.

I felt Tribulation deceived me by not telling me before marriage about his lifestyle. I also resented his "whatever" attitude and indifference to the effects his transvestite activity, addictions and psychological abuse had on my life.

I met a lady that talked with me about her experiences with her husband that was psychologically abusive to her. She left him thirty years earlier but had not forgiven him. She was diagnosed with an aggressive form of breast cancer and went to the Mayo Clinic for treatment. To her surprise someone at the Mayo Clinic discussed the connection between disease and not forgiving others. She advised me to forgive Tribulation, stating it would only hurt me if I did not. She died less then a year after her diagnosis.

I needed God's help to even make the first step (which is an act of my will) to forgive Tribulation. Anger was all I felt and I did not want to forgive at first. But after praying about this I read the scripture:

"For it is God which worketh in you both to will and to do of [his] good pleasure."
Philippians 2:13

God knows my heart's desire is always to honor and obey His word. And He knew forgiving Tribulation was very hard for me. I prayed scriptures out loud daily for several months, and have finally forgiven Tribulation.

Part Two

Fresh Start

Transformation

Fresh Start

Chapter Seven

Decisions

"He brought me up also out of an horrible pit, out of the miry clay, and set my feet upon a rock, [and] established my goings."
Psalm 40:2

By the time I was fifty years old, in 2008, I had been under the control and power of people who manipulated my mind, time and very life! After leaving the marriage, I felt like I had been in a fog going through life with things happening to me, but I was never present. I said to myself, "You can finally live now, whatever happens will depend totally on your own decisions. But now what?" New challenges were learning how to think, and live on my own. I began my new life in a bare apartment, children away in college, no friends and estranged from siblings. Feelings of sadness and pity for myself began to creep in.

"Religious" Activity

The word "religious" is in quotations in this book to describe outward traditions that replaced what should have been the real focus (**I Peter 3:3-4**). In church I was taught a saved person had to perform "religious" activity to be pleasing to God and to receive answered prayers. The list of "religious" activity include:

- Emotionalism is of great importance
- Crying loud to God
- Sin consciousness
- No make up
- No nail polish
- Long skirts
- Dollies on the head in church (females)
- Don't wear pants in church
- Closed toed shoes
- No short sleeves
- No haircuts (females)
- Don't dye hair
- Submit/obey leaders of the church
- Never miss a group/ church service (regardless of the reason)

New Church

To begin my new life, I joined a new church of the same denomination that also practiced "religious" activity. I obeyed the rules and gave away things that were seen as "sinful" or "unholy." Their "religious" activity added to the previous list:

- Pants (could not be worn at all)
- No Jewelry (except: cross necklace, broach, wedding ring, watch)
- No plaiting of hair/locks
- Sheer pantyhose (skin should not be seen through hose)
- Movie theatre attendance not allowed

After a year of performing "religious" activity to the best of my ability, the effects of the abuse from the past still lingered. I struggled day-to-day thinking, "What else can I do to get God to help me?" I cried out, "Where are you God?" "Why won't you make everything better?" I went to the library to find Christian books on the subject of recovery from abuse. I checked out books authored by several ministers. I flipped through each book looking for answers. Finding a book by Dr. Creflo A. Dollar led me to watch his messages on my computer (I did not own a television). Through his messages I learned that I was asking God the wrong questions. I was not asking questions that would invoke His intervention into my life. What I really wanted to know from God was how to I recover from the abusive past. While searching for answers to be healed, I continued to practice "religious" activity. The <u>process</u> of changing my thoughts about "religious" activity in order to receive from God took time.

Receiving God's Love

A book by Joyce Meyer, led me to watch her messages on the computer. Hearing Joyce describe freedom from an abusive past, I learned a person could be healed. I began to believe God was willing and able to help me work through the process of recovery. From Joyce Meyer I learned that God loves me and as I receive God's love fear would be driven out of my life.

"There is no fear in love; but perfect love casteth out fear: because fear hath torment."

I John 4:18

I was led to scriptures about God's love and learned that God was waiting on me to receive His love and believe His word.

"And we have known and believed the love that God hath to us. God is love..."
I John 4:16

The revelation that God loves me was overwhelming! In that "light bulb moment" I began the process of believing and receiving His love. This was the first step to recovering from my abusive past. I began to say out loud daily, "I believe God loves me." I learned that I needed to make a request to God based on His word and believe because He loves me He would answer. The Holy Spirit prompted me to read scriptures about God's love for people that was demonstrated through Jesus. He was always ready and willing to help anyone that asked.

"...A man full of leprosy: who seeing Jesus...besought him, saying, Lord, if thou wilt, thou canst make me clean...(Jesus) touched him, saying, I will: be thou clean. And immediately the leprosy departed from him."
Luke 5:12-13

Learning to Love myself

Growing in the knowledge that God loves me was a start to learning about love in every way. I was prompted to read other scriptures on the topic of love.

"And thou shalt love the Lord thy God with all thy heart, and with all thy soul, and with all thy mind, and with all thy strength: this [is] the first commandment. And the second [is] like, [namely] this, Thou shalt love thy neighbor as thyself. There is none other commandment greater than these."
Mark 12:30-31

The scripture says to love God with all my being and love people as myself. That was a powerful revelation. Love my neighbor as myself? How could I do that when I hated myself? I wasn't sure how to begin to follow the command of Jesus, as I didn't know how to love. I began to renew my mind with the word of God and meditate on the scriptures I was already reading about God's love for me. This began the journey of learning to love myself so I could follow Jesus' command to love God and love people as myself. I began first speaking praises to God expressing my love to Him.

"We love him, because he first loved us."
I John 4:19

Divorce

As stated in Chapter Two, I used credit cards to pay for daily life beyond my paycheck due to the lack of financial support from Tribulation. After separating from the marriage I was overwhelmed with over $51,000 credit card debt. Twice, in a year's time, I attempted Consumer Credit

Counseling to lower my payments to creditors but was unsuccessful. The credit agency advised me to file for bankruptcy relief. I needed to be on a payment plan with the court in order to pay the filing fees. I spoke scriptures out loud confessing and believing the promise of God's word that He would help me, as I did not have money for a lawyer.

"But the Comforter, [which is] the Holy Ghost, whom the Father will send in my name, he shall teach you all things…"
John 14:26

The bankruptcy filing process is complex and laborious and through the grace of God I was able to complete the process and receive a discharge of the credit card debt in 2009. God is great!

I then needed the Holy Spirit to teach and guided me through the divorce process. I had to save for several weeks to pay the filing fees. Books from the public library and the law library at the court were resources used to view copies of cases. I prayed over the information found and completed the documents for divorce. First, I filed for a limited divorce and created a separation agreement from a sample in a library book, and mailed it to Tribulation to be signed. He refused to sign the separation agreement and he was not served the papers for the limited divorce. I waited and believed by faith for the will of God to be done for my good in this situation. The Holy Spirit revealed to me that I needed an absolute divorce to dissolve the marriage and regain my birth last name. I saved money again to be able to file for absolute divorce on the grounds of constructive desertion and cruelty/excessive vicious conduct against me. Tribulation was served the papers for the absolute divorce and contested the divorce.

At the divorce hearing, the choices to present my case on the grounds filed or a "no fault" divorce were presented to me. Tribulation was prepared to fight over the ownership of the house. Thank God I had already surrendered the house in bankruptcy and had filed a quit deed claim with the court. As I stated in Chapter Two, I chose to love God more than the house. The promise of Jesus is:

"And Jesus answered and said, Verily I say unto you, There is no man that hath left house... for my sake, and the gospel's....But he shall receive an hundredfold now in this time, houses..."
Mark 10:29-30

In the end, I decided it was best to not go through a long trial, but chose a "no fault" divorce. I just wanted to move on with my life. Tribulation agreed to the "no fault" divorce. I did not have to pay him alimony and I kept my own pension, as he did his. The divorce was final in January 2010. Tribulation currently lives in the house today.

Chapter Eight

Work Experiences

"They shall not labour in vain, nor bring forth for trouble…"
Isaiah 65:23

I began a career as a vocal music educator the second year of the marriage. My first teaching job, Fillmore Arts Center (grades kindergarten through eighth), was a few blocks from my alma mater, Duke Ellington School of the Arts. I replaced a beloved teacher and was the first African-American vocal music teacher they ever had. Only one girl remained in the chorus, but before I transferred from that school, God blessed me with ideas to grow the chorus to 120 students. Throughout my career, every place I was employed, the previous vocal music teacher was beloved and students were resistant to working with me. God blessed me at each school providing ideas to enhance the music department in some area and in short time students willingly participated in the vocal music classes. The choruses received superior ratings at the county, state and national adjudications.

Challenging Environment

In 2010, I prayed for an opportunity to work at the high school level to help talented students prepare for college and receive scholarships. God provided me favor with people I did not know, who recommended me for a high school vocal music position in Beltsville, Maryland. The previous vocal music teacher was beloved by the students as was the case when I started at other schools, but this situation was different from the others. Christian parents and students who were resistant to me working at the school, joined together with Christian alumni to withstand the vision God had given me. One student sent me an unkind e-mail. Students were disruptive in class while I was teaching chorus even to the point of walking around the room and playing the piano as though I was not there.

As the county choral adjudication was required, I attended with the chorus. Students deliberately sang incorrectly on stage, and refused to participate in the sight-reading and sight singing adjudication. A student told me later, the students decided, I would not receive superior ratings that year as I had at previous schools. Not deterred by the students and parents, I prayed:

"Rid me, and deliver me from the hand of strange children, whose mouth speaketh vanity, and their right hand [is] a right hand of falsehood."
Psalm 144:11

The experiences with the people at the school helped me grow stronger in faith and belief in God's word. I believed that God was going to turn this negative environment into a blessing. I remembered that God had always been with me and these people could not stop His plan for my life. During this time, I learned how to lean totally on God to provide wisdom and guidance for every decision regarding this teaching assignment. One morning as I was praying before work, the Holy Spirit led me to:

"...Not by might, nor by power, but by my spirit, saith the LORD of hosts."
Zechariah 4:6

This scripture gave me peace and confidence that the Spirit of God was going to manifest a positive outcome in this situation to the glory of God.

Favor of God

Many of the resistant chorus students signed up for the countywide high school honors chorus and needed my permission to participate, I gave my consent. They wanted to work with a friend of their former chorus teacher after school. That same year, the vocal music supervisor invited me to be one of the countywide elementary honors chorus directors. The elementary and high schools along with the middle school were to perform at the same venue. This was an annual Prince Georges' County Public Schools honors chorus series at the John F. Kennedy Center for the Performing Arts in Washington, D.C.

As I prayed for guidance of the selections I would conduct, the Holy Spirit led me to compose a song (I have been a composer for many years). When I prayed for an idea, the Holy Spirit reminded me that this was the 35th Anniversary of this event and led me to the scripture:

"O GIVE thanks unto the LORD; for [he is] good: because his mercy [endureth] for ever."
Psalm 118:1

The melody to this scripture came to me a few days later while I was asleep and within one week the song was complete. The vocal music supervisor listened to the song and approved the song's performance at the concert. God provided me the opportunity to conduct this song at the Kennedy Center for the Performing Arts while the students and parents from my high school looked on. The performance of the song received a standing ovation from the audience. A few years later, I was invited to be one of the high school honors chorus directors. God blessed me to conduct one of my compositions, "Gloria A Swahili Praise Song." It was performed at the Clarice Smith Center at the University of Maryland.

"By this I know that thou favourest me, because mine enemy doth not triumph over me."
Psalm 41:11

Guitar Program
At the end of my first year at the high school, only a few students were signing up for my classes for the next year. I was told that visual art classes might be assigned to me. I said to the Lord, "I can't draw." He said to me, "I know that, why don't you offer guitar classes, and I will help you."

"...The LORD thy God shall bless thee in all thy works, and in all that thou puttest thine hand unto."
Deuteronomy 15:10

I needed administrative approval to offer a class that was not on the normal list of music courses. Approval was given on a trial basis to see if anyone would sign up. I was confident that students would sign up because this was God's plan. One hundred and twenty-nine students that signed up for the one class, God is great! Administration gave approval for a new course to be added to the music curriculum at the school and six classes of guitar were scheduled and filled to capacity. I prayed for wisdom and guidance to teach a subject of which I had limited experience. Without fail as I inquired of God, He showed me what and how to teach. I was led me to resources and people that made this class a success!

"Call unto me, and I will answer thee, and shew thee great and mighty things, which thou knowest not."
Jeremiah 33:3

God opened the door for me to teach students that had never enrolled in a music class and gave me interaction with the general school population. Guitar classes were added to the regular music course offerings. The music curriculum was expanded and the principal needed to hire another vocal music teacher. The guitar program grew to students participating in the county and state guitar adjudications where they received superior ratings. I was prompted to compose a song for chorus in the Spanish language with guitar accompaniment that was performed at a national competition. The guitar student's performance received the outstanding accompanist award in Pennsylvania. God is so good!

And It Came to Pass

Within a year at the high school I met the most wonderful and supportive Christian and Non-Christian parents and students in my life and career. One day when I returned from being absent, students asked where I was and said they missed me. I replied, "Sure you did!" Several students pulled me to the side and told me they were sincere. They said, "We really miss you when you are not here! We love you and appreciate how you teach and respect us as students." I began to observe their interactions with one another and saw that they were genuine caring, and loving people. I had to learn how to accept and receive their kindness.

My second year at the high school the students demonstrated support to the vision God had given me by hard work, willingness to try new things and attendance at performances. The parents transported students to county and state festivals, performances at Wolf Trap and National Harbor just to name a few. Most of the guitar student's parents had not participated in music events or traveled to music festivals and performances, but willing did so. Students were willing to learn the songs God gave me to compose in Hebrew, Swahili, and other languages.

I was not aware that students were impacted by the fact that I composed music until two students talked with me about the songs they had composed. I listened to their songs and they were quite good! My prayers to impact students in order to help them prepare for college and receive scholarships were answered by the great grace of God. A student submitted a song she composed in a competition at Full Sail University and won the Creative Minds Scholarship where she is now a Recording Arts major. Other students were successful as well. One student was accepted at the Berklee College of music as a vocal Jazz major. Another student the first in her family to complete high school (others had only completed 10th grade) is attending Morgan State University majoring in music on university and Maryland State Delegate scholarships.

"[But] verily God hath heard [me]; he hath attended to the voice of my prayer."
Psalm 66:19

Award

I received a phone call from the assistant vocal music supervisor for my county. She said I had been nominated for a national outstanding music educator award. She informed me that I had to submit an information package about myself to complete the process. Of the nearly three hundred nominations submitted from forty-five states, only fifty teachers would be selected.

By God's great grace I was selected to be a 2013 Yale Distinguished Music Educator. This award included an all expenses paid trip to Yale University. Four days of workshops, discussions, and other events concluded with a banquet and receiving of certificate. I thank God for the opportunity to be a demonstration of His great goodness, faithfulness and love!

"For thou, LORD, hast made me glad through thy work: I will triumph in the works of thy hands."
Psalm 92:4

Retirement

After four years at the high school and twenty-eight years of teaching, I inquired of God whether to continue in my profession. I began teaching while married to have income having never inquired of God what my calling is. I want to be sure to fulfill the purpose of God for my life. I was prompted to attend a county retirement workshop and followed the steps toward retirement. As the date neared to retire, I continued to work with students to achieve success. That year, at adjudication, the guitar, chamber chorus and vocal solo students all received superior ratings at the county level. Vocal solo, one guitar student and chamber chorus received excellent ratings at adjudication at the state level. And one guitar student received superior ratings at adjudication at the state level.

Looking back on my career as a vocal music educator, I grew in understanding of the great grace and love of God for me as He demonstrated it through success after success. He provided me great grace, and wisdom to create lesson plans, compose music, write curriculum, course outlines, create Student Learning Objectives Exemplars (SLO) for my county, adjudicate chorus festival in another county, adjudicate All State auditions, be a mentor teacher, create Arts Integration lessons, and much more. I give God all the glory for the things He has done!

"For he that is mighty hath done to me great things; and holy [is] his name."
Luke 1:49

Transformation

Chapter Nine

True Prosperity

"...Be ye transformed by the renewing of your mind, that ye may prove what [is] that good, and acceptable, and perfect, will of God."
Romans 12:2

I didn't know and therefore was not experiencing all the benefits that Jesus died and rose from the dead to provide for me as a born again believer. Christian people I knew were not experiencing the benefits either. Everyone was talking about how busy the devil is and how bad things are as though that were our plight in life. Through Dr. Creflo A. Dollar's Ministry, I was introduced to Kenneth Copland Ministries (KCM) and began watching the KCM broadcast in 2009. On "The Believer's Voice of Victory" telecast Kenneth Copland Ministries discussed Christians being whole in Jesus Christ. Brother Copland said the Christian life should not be hard, we should not be struggling and being defeated. He said "Because you're a born again child of Almighty God, you can rise above circumstances." Brother Copland read Galatians 3 and said, when Jesus took on the curse for all of mankind, He made available The Blessing. Which is wholeness in every area of our lives: spirit, soul (mind, will, emotions), body (health/wellness)

I Thessalonians 5:23, financial III John 1:2, and relational prosperity Romans 12:4-5. The Blessing also has protection and safety benefits II Timothy 4:18.

"Christ hath redeemed us from the curse of the law...That the blessing of Abraham might come on the Gentiles through Jesus Christ...And if ye [be] Christ's, then are ye Abraham's seed, and heirs according to the promise."
Galatians 3:13-14; 29

Brother Copland said just being born again will not make true prosperity happen in life. He said, "Faith begins when the will of God is known." All of the promises and the way to receive them are in the Bible. A person will need to spend time in the word, release faith, apply it by doing what is says, confess it by speaking it as your own and praise God as though it is already done. I learned from KCM that in order to see the manifestation of The Blessing I must "Call those things which be not as thought they were" Romans 4:17. Speaking what God says about the situation will make it manifest in life. I was saying what I had and getting more of the same not realizing I get what I say (Matthew 12:37). This is an important point and the Bible confirms this through out. Also, faith with patience is required (Hebrews 6:12). I learned patience does not mean to put up something, but to remain steady in God.

Spiritual Prosperity

I had already received the first step to true prosperity by being born again and had the Holy Spirit. Although I was reading the word of God and experiencing some results, I learned that the power is in praying God's words, not makeup my own (**Isaiah 58:13**). Pray the answer, God's promises, not the problem. I also needed a revelation of the word to live a life of victory everyday. I had to believe on the inside that true prosperity and all the promises of God and His goodness belong to me.

"For all the promises of God in him [are] yea, and in him Amen, unto the glory of God by us."
II Corinthians 1:20

Financial Prosperity

I had a poor person's image and mindset on the inside that manifested on the outside into barely making ends meet each month. I began to renew my mind with the word of God to change that image when I read Deuteronomy 28 of the blessing and the curse. Financial needs met are under the blessing, lack and not enough are under the curse. I searched for scriptures to learn about the blessing of Abraham. The will of God is for His people to have financial resources in abundance as to have more than enough in order to give to others.

"... I will bless thee...and thou shalt be a blessing."
Genesis 12:3

I learned to change my conversation of always talking about what I did not have and saying that I could not afford something. I became aware through KCM that words are very important. I began to confess God's words over my finances:

"The LORD shall increase you more and more, you and your children."
Psalm 115:14

Financial Miracle

In 2009, my car had mechanical difficulties and made a lot of noise. The dealership told me the exhaust system needed repair at the cost of $2,000. I did not have the money, continued to drive it everyday, and prayed for a miracle. After two weeks the car would not shift into gear. As I prayed for wisdom and guidance, the Holy Spirit led me to have the car towed to the dealership and to call my car insurance company. When the dealership tested the car they said, "Someone has stolen your catalytic converter." The insurance company paid over $2,000 for the repairs and my cost was a $100.00 deductible. God is good! The manifestation of The Blessing was beginning!

Peace in My Soul

I worried constantly about every thing all my life. I thought it was normal to worry about things until I learned that when I worry I am not trusting God. Faith is based on confidence in God to work on my behalf. Confidence is assurance, resting, and knowing through faith.

Worry is fear-based thoughts trying to figure out by using human reasoning to solve a problem. I was mentally and physically worn out most of the time from worry. Worry produced confusion in my mind and emotions. I was creating problems I did not have to deal with if I would believe God, listen to the Holy Spirit and follow His instructions.

"Peace I leave with you, my peace I give unto you: not as the world giveth, give I unto. Let not your heart be troubled, neither let it be afraid."
John 14:27

Peaceable Outcome

I constantly worried about my children in college. I was concerned about them maintaining good grades in order to keep their scholarships. I wondered if they would graduate and be able to get a job upon graduation in order to support themselves. I had to stop worrying and have confidence in God's ability, and the Holy Spirit in them that is working to bring to pass The Blessing in their lives.

Whatever challenges they had in college, The Blessing was always working to bring a positive outcome. Both children excelled in college in leadership and community opportunities. My daughter was Vice President of Alpha Nu Omega, Sorority, Inc. in 2009 and Marketing Intern for the Washington National Opera in 2010. My son was named one the Most Influential NYU students of 2011 for cofounding the Black Student Union and received the NYU Presidential Award in 2012. Both children graduated from college, were employed before graduation and are living on their own. The Blessing continues to protect and provide for them everyday. I learned from Gloria Copland that a born again believer has covenant promises from God concerning their children. One scripture she uses to teach on this subject is:

"Thus saith the LORD; Refrain thy voice from weeping, and thine eyes from tears: for thy work shall be rewarded, saith the LORD; and they [your children] shall come again from the land of the enemy. And there is hope in thine end, saith the LORD, that thy children shall come again to their own border."
Jeremiah 31:16-17

Protection

KCM taught another component of The Blessing the believers have is protection. Brother Copland preached a sermon about the believer's authority by faith in Jesus Name over storms.

"Then he (Jesus) arose, and rebuked the wind and the raging of the water: and they ceased, and there was a calm. And he (Jesus) said unto them, Where is your faith?"
Luke 8:24-25

I speak daily confessions over my children and myself everyday like Psalm 91 and others. There are scriptures that explain that we have Heavenly angels to enforce the word of God that we speak:

"Bless the LORD, ye his angels, that excel in strength, that do his commandments, hearkening unto the voice of his word."
Psalm 103:20

Hurricane Sandy

All of the news and weather telecasts were predicting the massive storm Sandy and the destruction they expected it to bring. Upon hearing that forecast, I refused to get in fear and stop my faith from working for protection especially for my children. I got my Bible and concordance to looked up all the scriptures I could find on protection and protection from storms. One of them is:

"He maketh the storm a calm, so that the waves thereof are still. Then are they glad because they be quiet..."
Psalm 107:29-30

I wrote down scriptural prayers putting my children's names in them and posted them all over my apartment walls. When the storm hit, October 2012, I closed the blinds, walked through each room and read the scriptures out loud. Prayed in the Spirit for help in areas I may not know what to pray:

"Likewise the Spirit also helpeth our infirmities: for we know not what we should pray for as we ought: but the Spirit itself maketh intercession for us with groanings which cannot be uttered."
Romans 8:26

When the storm was over my daughter's lights did not go out in Maryland. Her car and apartment were not damaged and she got paid time off from work after the storm. My son's lights in Brooklyn,

New York did not go out. There was no water damage in his area and he got paid time off after the storm. I heard other people's stories of God's protection during Hurricane Sandy. God is no respecter of persons, He responds to faith and trust in His word.

"God [is] not a man, that he should lie...hath he said, and shall he not do [it]? or hath he spoken, and shall he not make it good?"
Numbers 23:19

Health/Wellness

Living without physical or mental health issues was not something I had experienced. My inside image was as a sick person. Before I heard the message about The Blessing, I was not sure that I could or was suppose to live a healthy life. The idea of wellness was a new concept to me, but I took hold of it. I began to change the self-image by speaking the word, believing that it is God's will for me to live without sickness and disease.

"...Jesus Christ maketh thee whole: arise, and make thy bed. And he arose immediately."
Acts 9:34

Answer to Health Challenge

In 2010, I began having symptoms of numbness in my hands, feet and legs, weakness, and memory loss. The doctor ordered multiple tests but could not find the cause. As I prayed for wisdom and guidance the Holy Spirit revealed the symptoms were side effects of the PPIs I was taking for GERD.

I immediately stopped taking the medication and became very ill then I resumed to take the PPIs. As I continued to pray for wisdom, I was prompted to ask a pharmacist for advice. He explained that most medication, especially any that has had long term use has to be weaned off. After three months I was weaned off the PPIs, and able to eat for the first time in twenty years without medication. And the other symptoms subsided completely. Praise Jesus! Later, I read an article that confirmed one of the side effects of PPIs is B12 deficiency that produces the symptoms I was experiencing. The article is: Harvard Health Publications: Harvard Medical School; "Do PPIs have long-term side effects?" The Family Health Guide; February 2009.

Relational Prosperity

Developing relationships with others was a challenge for me. I had to change my inner image of being alone, to see myself interacting with others. I needed wisdom of how to proceed in this area, as I did not want to open the door to unhealthy relationships.

"If any of you lack wisdom, let him ask of God, that giveth to all [men] liberally, and upbraideth not; and it shall be given him."
James 1:5

Opportunity to Develop

In 2013, I moved from my apartment due to a tenant's drug activity and the resident manager's refusal to resolve the issue. I moved within a twenty-four hour period as I was becoming physically ill from the smell of cooked crack cocaine. This is the second time in my life I gave everything away except a few clothes, shoes. This time I kept one piece of furniture, a small chest that I liked. With limited resources (due to the fees for breaking a lease) and nowhere else to go, I went to live with my older sister in Washington, D.C. where I was born and raised.

As I stated in another chapter, she and I were working on having a positive relationship due to past history. The move to her place fast-forwarded the process of being more than just tolerant of one another. This was an uncomfortable situation for me as I slept on her sofa in the living room, at the foot of her fifty-five gallon fish tank, and special frog tank. She took medication for Obsessive Compulsive Disorder (OCD) and was trying very hard not to loose her temper when I did not do everything exactly the way she liked it.

I increased my prayer time, confessions of God's word and listening to CD and DVD messages of KCM. Maintaining focus that this was only a temporary situation was a challenge at times. Determined not to slip back into old thought patterns of worry, fear, and depression. Every evening after work, before entering my sister's condo, I recited the KCM "Confession of Victory Over Defeat" prayer (see prayer from KCM website). I believe that God is always good and living like this was not His best for me.

"He staggered not at the promise of God through unbelief; but was strong in faith, giving glory to God."

Romans 4:20

I used headphones to played music in my ears all night to block out the fish tank sound. I literally praised God in song all night. When thoughts of defeat entered my mind, I cast them down in the Name of Jesus (**II Corinthians 10:3-5**). Everyday I inquired of God where to move, and believed Him for the provision to bring it to pass.

After three months, I was led to an apartment five blocks from my sister's place. I was thankful to have my own place again. It is walking distance from the metro subway and the bus. Living in D.C. again gives me the opportunity to experience things I missed out on in my childhood, like walking in the neighborhood without fear.

The time living with my sister was valuable to our relationship and it helped me see myself in a different light. I became less isolated in my thinking. I had to because she has a lot of friends that dropped by all hours of the day and night. I began to not resent their visits as violating my space but watched how she interacted with people. Today, I have developed my own relationships with people seeing through my sibling the scripture:

"A man [that hath] friends must shew himself friendly: and there is a friend [that] sticketh closer than a brother."
Proverbs 18:24

Chapter Ten

Life Today

"Ye are of God, little children, and have overcome them: because greater is he that is in you, than he that is in the world."
I John 4:4

I am an overcomer, and past circumstances cannot define who I am today. I read my Bible everyday and pray to the Father in the Name of Jesus. I inquire of God for every detail of my life. I also listen or watch a message everyday of KCM or partner ministries. This way I learn more about God, renew my mind and feed my spirit as I develop, **"from faith to faith"** (**Romans 1:17**). This week, my study is "My Sheep Hear My Voice" from Keith Moore Ministries. When difficult days come, I remind myself that I am already an overcomer and **"No weapon that is formed against thee shall prosper..."** (**Isaiah 54:17**).

Get Results

When challenges come in life I follow the advice of Brother Copland in the August 2015 Believer's Voice of Victory (BVOV) Magazine. The article is titled "Riding Above the Storm." He said, "You don't ever have to be under the circumstances. You don't have to just hunker down under their onslaught, like the rest of the world does, and do your best to make it through. You can ride in victory over every storm. Here are some points to get you there:"

1. Take refuge in the Name of the One who is far greater than any storm. **Proverbs 18:10: "The name of the LORD is a strong tower: the righteous runneth into it, and is safe."**

2. Believe in that Name and use it to exercise authority over the devil. **Mark 16:17: "And these signs shall follow them that believe; In my name shall they cast out devils..."**

3. Remember that this is not optional, God has commanded you to do it. **First John 3:23: "...This is his commandment, That we should believe on the name of his Son Jesus Christ, and love one another..."**

4. The Name Jesus inherited through His work of redemption is God's own Name and there is none greater. **Philippians 2:9-10: "Wherefore God also hath highly exalted him, and given him a name which is above every name: that at the name of Jesus every knee should bow, of things in heaven, and things in earth, and things under the earth."**

5. As a joint heir with Christ, that Name belongs to you just as surely as it belongs to Jesus. **Ephesians 3:14-15 "For this cause I bow my knees unto the Father of our Lord Jesus Christ, of whom the whole family in heaven and earth is named."**

Resist Old Mindsets

The devil <u>tries</u> to employ old mindsets of depression, feeling sorry for oneself, symptoms of sickness and disease to steal the growth that has been accomplished. He is always looking for a way to **"steal, kill and destroy."** <u>**John 10:10**</u> The devil makes suggestions to try to get the person to take or accept his ideas as true instead of the word of God. Once the person accepts the idea, fear, the old mindset then he little by little brings about the negative results.

Speaking the word of God about circumstances and situations is key. Speaking the negative situation only enforces more of the same. I heard Dr. Creflo A. Dollar say, "The <u>fact</u> might be that symptoms are present in the body, but the <u>truth</u> is **Jesus bore our sickness so by His stripes we are healed (Isaiah 53:4-5)**". He went on to say, "We must see ourselves not as the sick trying to get well. We are the well protecting our health against sickness and disease."

I learned how to resist old mindsets by focusing on a promise of God and saying out loud, "The word of God is true about my situation, and anything else is a lie." Then I surround myself with teaching CDs, DVDs, books and songs of praise to drive out the negative thoughts, by replacing them with the Word of God.

"Submit yourselves therefore to God. Resist the devil, and he will flee from you."
James 4:7

Keep the Victory

Maintaining the word of God in the eyes, ears, and mouth until it gets it down in the heart is important to keep victory in life (**Proverbs 4:20-22**). Through reading the word everyday I learned how to recognize the voice of God when He speaks to my heart. Being sensitive to the promptings of the Holy Spirit and praying in the Spirit everyday is important. The Holy Spirit knows all things and reveals what is unknown. The ability to interpret is available to anyone.

"...Pray that he may interpret..."
I Corinthians 14:13

I do not get literal interpretations most times when I pray in the Spirit but promptings and take action accordingly. An example of this is when my daughter told me she and friends were going on a trip. I was prompted by the Spirit of scriptures to write in a scriptural prayer petition for safety. On their way back home, the plane had mechanical difficulties and landed unexpectedly. When she text me about the problem, I had an unusual peace and read the prayer petition out loud. I told her all was going to be well. Within thirty minutes the flight resumed and they got home safely. Praise Jesus!

I also found joy to be an important factor in my daily life. There are many scriptures that instruct Christians to have joy and rejoice (**Philippians 4:4**). Joy is different from happiness. Happiness is based on feelings or circumstances. Joy is based on what I know and believe. One of the ways to get a good laugh is through Christian comedians, and comedies on television. But the best way is to focus on scriptures that describe victory in Jesus (**I John 5:4-5**). I laugh by faith even when I don't feel like it. When I meditate on these scriptures, I laugh and laugh until I have a good belly laugh!

"A merry heart doeth good [like] a medicine..."
Proverbs 17:22

Partaking of Food

Starting in 2008, most of my time was used to focus on nourishing my spirit and soul. I neglected my body's need for nourishment through food. I was eating more than in the past but still had the mindset of it as something difficult to do regularly. Over the years I developed a self-reliant attitude due to interaction with the abusers in my past. My self-effort to gain victory in the area of eating only produced frustration.

In 2014, I released the care of the eating disorder to God and began to trust the grace of God to help me. As I understand it, grace is God's unearned, unmerited favor (**Ephesians 2:8**). Faith is the channel by which grace is available (**Romans 4:16**). The bible says God has given to every man the measure of faith (**Romans 12:3**). Faith grows when it is fed the Word of God daily (**Romans 10:17**) and Jesus is the author and finisher of faith (**Hebrews 12:2**). Faith along with patience (remain the same, steady), produce results (**Hebrews 6:12**). The bible says grace is given to believers (**Ephesians 4:7**) as a gift (**Ephesians 3:7**). Grace is available to those who humble themselves to receive it (**I Peter 5:5**) and He is the God of all grace (**I Peter 5:10**).

When I released the eating disorder to the grace of God, I felt like a weight was lifted off my shoulders. The Holy Spirit revealed to me that I needed to see myself eating, enjoying food and believe that this is the will of God for me. I needed to be set free in my mind first in this area before it could manifest in my life.

> **"...My grace is sufficient for thee: for my strength is made perfect in weakness..."**
> **II Corinthians 12:9**

I created a scriptural prayer regarding eating and called the KCM prayer line. The prayer partner agreed with me regarding deliverance and gave me additional scriptures to use as prayers. I am now free in my mind regarding food. I eat several times a day, enjoy planning meals and going out with my friends to eat. Today, I am blessed to have hunger pains. But when I ignore them, the desire to eat decreases for several days. When I feel hunger pains and respond by eating, the desire increases as well as the ability to eat a variety of foods. Glory to God! At mealtime I pray:

> **"...Meats (foods), which God hath created to be received with thanksgiving of them which believe and know the truth...for it is sanctified by the word of God and prayer."**
> **I Timothy 4:3; 5**

Believing God for a House

In 2009, in my prayer time, God made three specific promises to me that at the time seemed impossible to come to pass:

"And I have been with thee withersoever thou hast walked, and have cut off all thine enemies from before thee, and have made thee a name like the name of the great men that [are] in the earth...furthermore I tell thee that the LORD will build thee an house."
I Chronicles 17:8; 10

The first promise came to pass when the divorce was final in 2010 and Tribulation finally stopped threatening and contacting me. The second promise came to pass in 2013 when I received the Yale University Distinguished Music Educator Award. I expect the third promise of owning a house will also come to pass in Jesus' Name. I believe God will provide a house for me debt free. It is not a sin to borrow money but after my experience of filing bankruptcy, borrowing money is not for me! The Bible is true:

"... The borrower [is] servant to the lender."
Proverbs 22:7

I read testimonies by KCM partners in the BVOV magazine of people who bought houses debt free. Here are few examples. One lady's business supernaturally prospered and she bought two houses debt free. One for herself and another for someone else! Another lady was prompted to speak with a builder of new houses about purchasing. God gave her favor with the builder and he allowed her to make payments and plan/design her house at the same time. God also gave her favor with her employer and she received several raises in pay. When the house was complete she was able to move into the house debt free. God has many ways of bringing to pass His promises. He is only limited when I limit Him. And I am taking the limits off in Jesus Name!

As I inquire of God for the wisdom, and the manifestation of my house, I will enjoy each day He has given me and remind myself:

"But seek ye first the kingdom of God, and his righteousness; and all these things shall be added unto you."
Matthew 6:33

Another Church

My partnership with KCM opened my eyes to new freedoms in Christ Jesus and in 2013, I was finally ready to be rid of all "religious" activity. I wanted to be free in my style of dress and enjoy other things in life. I searched for a new church using the KCM web site to look for ministries in my area that were partners with KCM. After several weeks of visiting a different church each Sunday, I joined a church where most of the members came out of churches that had a lot of "religious" activity and traditions, and are in search of more of the word of God. After a few months I was prompted to withdraw my membership because it was not where I belong. Then I attended another church with the focus on love and fellowship but was prompted to continue my search for a church home. In 2015, I joined a church three blocks from my apartment. I enjoy that the focus of the church is prayer, worship and service to others.

Conclusion

One of the most life changing revelations I received from Brother Copland is "When we walk and live by faith, we never have to change our lifestyle because of the times." As I understand it that means if I have $2.00 or $2,000,000 in the bank I depend on God. I trust Him for everything that pertains to life and godliness (**II Peter 1:3**).

"...The just shall live by faith."
Galatians 3:11

I was prompted by the Holy Spirit to take early retirement in July 2014 at age fifty-five to complete my first book "Overcoming the Effects of Abuse through Scriptural Prayers: A Memoir of Faith, Healing and Transformation." It was published in October 2014. My retirement pay is a fraction of my salaried income so walking by faith is essential. On December 31, 2014 I was prompted to read **Joel 2:21-27**. This scripture talks about restoration of the things lost and abundance. Based on that scripture, I declare daily that 2015 is my year of restoration and abundance in every area of my life (**Psalm 65:11**). God is taking care me in supernatural ways. An example is; my previous employer owed me a stipend of $1,500 from the year 2013, I received it in the mail in July 2015.

Encouragement and inspiration to others is my goal everyday. I purchase KCM materials and give them to others as the Holy Spirit directs me. I have given away numerous LifeLine 10-day Spiritual Action Plan Kits for Healing, Faith, Answered Prayers and Relationships (see KCM resources page). I gave an Answered Prayers Spiritual Action Plan Kit to a lady who had a legal problem. The next day she received a phone call from the judge in the case and received favor to have case dismissed. I have sowed multiple KCM books, CDs, DVDs. I have also sowed other partner ministry materials to people. I gave one such to a resident in my apartment building who was wheelchair bound, had limited mobility and speech. She had an attendant with her 24 hours a day. Several months after sowing this resource, I missed seeing her outside and asked her mother how she was doing. Her mother reported that her daughter (who is an adult) had moved out of the apartment and was living on her own elsewhere without an attendant. Her mother was thankful I had given her the materials, and said, "We expect her to walk any day now." Praise Jesus!

In July 2015, I was prompted to begin in music ministry. Months before I received the prompting on Valentine's Day 2015, someone gave me a new IPod and ITunes card to purchase music. When seeking the wisdom of God in regard to this ministry I was prompted to read:

"Let the word of Christ dwell in you richly in all wisdom; teaching and admonishing one another

in psalms and hymns and spiritual songs, singing with grace in your hearts to the Lord."
Colossians 3:16

I sing at nursing homes, homes of those recovering from illness and have been invited to sing at community events.

I know my life is just beginning and expect to live long, strong and prosperous until Jesus comes or until I am satisfied by living out the full number of my days. The way I see it, at least fifty more good years will make up for past fifty bad years, in Jesus' Name! I believe for this scripture to be fulfilled in me:

"They shall still bring forth fruit in old age; they shall be fat and flourishing; To shew that the LORD [is] upright: [he is] my rock, and [there is] no unrighteousness in him."
Psalm 92:14-15

Part Three

A Scriptural Prayer

Self Help

KCM Resources

Chapter Eleven

A Scriptural Prayer

"... Go in peace: and the God of Israel grant [thee]
thy petition that thou hast asked of him."
I Samuel 1:17

Thank You Heavenly Father in the Name of Jesus.
Wednesday, July 29, 2015 @6:18 am

Heavenly Father in the Name of Jesus,
Thank You for being my God **Joel 2:27**.
Thank You for Jesus my Lord **I Corinthians 12:3**.
Thank You for the Holy Spirit, my Comforter,
Counselor, Helper, Strengthener, Guide,
Intercessor and Advocate **John 15:26**.Thank You for
Heavenly help, my angels **Hebrews 1:13-14.**

This day, every day forward and forever, I choose
Your words, Your way of the Kingdom of God
Matthew 6:33.
I am Yours to command, Sir. Your will, Your plan be
done in my life, in Jesus' Name **John 14:10.**

I choose Life, I choose The Blessing in Jesus' Name.
Deuteronomy 30:19 "...Therefore choose life, that
both thou and thy seed may live."
I choose **Colossians 3:22** "...In singleness of heart,
fearing God." **Ephesians 6:5-6** "...Singleness of
your heart, as unto Christ...as servants of Christ,
doing the will of God from the heart."

I choose **Mark 16:15** "**Go ye into all the world, and preach The gospel to every creature.**"
I choose **I John 3:23** "**And this is his commandment, that we should believe on the name of his Son Jesus Christ, and love one another, as he gave us commandment.**"
I choose **Psalm 12:6** "**The words of the LORD are pure words: as silver tried in a furnace of earth, purified seven times.**"
I choose **Acts 4:29-30** "**...That with all boldness they may speak thy word. By stretching forth thine hand to heal: and that signs and wonders may be done by the name of thy holy child Jesus.**"

Therefore, I believe, I receive **Acts 4:33-34** "**And with great power gave the apostles witness of the resurrection of the Lord Jesus: and great grace was upon them all. Neither was there any among them that lacked.**" **Proverbs 10:22** "**The blessing of the LORD, it maketh rich, and he addeth no sorrow with it.**"

I pray this in Jesus' Name, and Lord I praise You. Amen

Priscilla Coleman

Chapter Twelve

Self-Help

Scripture Topics Alphabetized

"…He who blesseth himself in the earth shall bless himself in the God of truth…"
Isaiah 65:16

Angels

Genesis 32:1
"And Jacob went on his way, and the angels of God met him."
Exodus 14:19
"And the angel of God, which went before the camp of Israel, removed and went behind them; and the pillar of the cloud went from before their face, and stood behind them."
Exodus 23:20
"Behold, I send and Angel before thee, to keep thee in the way, and to bring thee into the place which I have prepared."
II Kings 6:16-17
"And he answered, Fear not: for they that [be] with us [are] more than they that [be] with them. And Elisha prayed, and said, LORD, I pray thee, open his eyes, that he may see. And the LORD opened the eyes of the young man; and he saw: and, behold,

the mountain [was] full of horses and chariots of fire round about Elisha."

Daniel 3:28

"[Then] Nebuchadnezzar spake, and said, Blessed [be] the God of Shadrach, Meshach, and Abednego, who hath sent his angel, and delivered his servants that trusted in him, and have changed the king's word, and yielded their bodies, that they might not serve nor worship any god, except their own God."

Psalm 34:7

"The angel of the LORD encampeth round about them that fear (honor) him, and delivereth them."

Psalm 91:11-12

"For he shall give his angels charge over thee, to keep thee in all thy ways. They shall bear thee up in [their] hands, lest thou dash thy foot against a stone."

Psalm 103:20

"Bless the LORD, ye his angels, that excel in strength, that do his commandments, hearkening unto the voice of his word."

Matthew 4:11

"Then the devil leaveth him, and, behold, angels came and ministered unto him."

Matthew 18:10

"Take heed that ye despise not one of these little ones; for I say unto you, That in heaven their angels do always behold the face of my Father which is in heaven."

Luke 1:28

"And the angel came in unto her, and said, Hail (Rejoice), [thou that art] highly favoured, the Lord [is] with thee: blessed [art] thou among women."

Luke 2:10

"And the angel said unto them, Fear not: for, behold, I bring you good tidings of great joy, which shall be to all people."

Luke 22:43

"And there appeared an angel unto him from heaven, strengthening him."

Acts 12:11

"And when Peter was come to himself, he said, Now I know of a surety, that the Lord hath sent his angel, and hath delivered me out of the hand of Herod…"

Acts 27:23

"For there stood by me this night the angel of God…"

Hebrews 1:13-14

"But to which of the angels said he at any time, Sit on my right hand, until I make thine enemies thy footstool? Are they not all ministering spirits, sent forth to minister for them who shall be heirs of salvation?"

Hebrews 13:2

"Be not forgetful to entertain strangers: for thereby some have entertained angels unawares."

Jude 1:9

"Yet Michael the archangel, when contending with the devil he disputed about the body of Moses, durst not bring against him a railing accusation, but said, The Lord rebuke thee."

Baptism

Matthew 3:13
"Then cometh Jesus from Galilee to Jordan unto John, to be baptized of him."

Mark 16:16
"He that believeth and is baptized shall be saved; but he that believeth not shall be damned."

John 1:33
"...He that sent me to baptize with water, the same said unto me, Upon whom thou shalt see the Spirit descending, and remaining on him, the same is he which baptizeth with the Holy Ghost."

Acts 2:38
"Then Peter said unto them, Repent, and be baptized every one of you in the name of Jesus Christ for the remission of sins, and ye shall receive the gift of the Holy Ghost."

Acts 8:36
"...See, [here is] water; what doth hinder me to be baptized?"

Acts 11:16
"Then remembered I the word of the Lord, how that he said, John indeed baptized with water; but ye shall be baptized with the Holy Ghost."

Acts 16:33
"...And was baptized, he and all his, straightway."

Acts 19:4-5
"The said Paul, John verily baptized with the baptism of repentance, saying unto the people, that they should believe on him which should come after him, that is, on Christ Jesus. When they heard [this], they were baptized in the name of the Lord Jesus."

Acts 22:16

"And now why tarriest thou? arise, and be baptized, and wash away thy sins, calling on the name of the Lord."

Romans 6:4

"Therefore we are buried with him by baptism into death: that like as Christ was raised up from the dead by the glory of the Father, even so we also should walk in newness of life."

I Corinthians 12:13

"For by one Spirit are we all baptized into one body..."

Colossians 2:12

"Buried with him in baptism, wherein also ye are risen with [him] through the faith of the operation of God, who hath raised him from the dead."

Galatians 3:27

"For as many of you as have been baptized into Christ have put on Christ."

Romans 6:3-4

"Know ye not, that so many of us as were baptized into Jesus Christ were baptized into his death? Therefore we are buried with him by baptism into death: that like as Christ was raised up from the dead by the glory of the Father, even so we also should walk in newness of life."

Blood Covenant/New Testament

Zechariah 9:11
"As for thee also, by the blood of thy covenant I have sent forth thy prisoners out of the pit wherein [is] no water."

Matthew 26:28
"For this is my blood of the new testament, which is shed for many for the remission of sins."

John 19:34
"But one of the soldiers with a spear pierced his side, and forthwith came there out blood and water."

I John 5:6
"This is he that came by water and blood, [even] Jesus Christ; not by water only, but by water and blood. And it is the Spirit that beareth witness, because the Spirit is truth."

Acts 17:26
"And hath made of one blood all nations of men for to dwell on all the face of the earth, and hath determined the times before appointed, and the bounds of their habitations."

Acts 20:28
"Take heed therefore unto yourselves, and to all the flock, over the which the Holy Ghost hath made you overseers, to feed the church of God, which he hath purchased with his own blood."

Romans 3:25
"Whom God hath set forth [to be] a propitiation through faith in his blood..."

Romans 5:9
"Much more then, being now justified by his blood, we shall be saved from wrath through him."

I Corinthians 10:16
"The cup of blessing which we bless, is it not the communion of the blood of Christ? The bread which we break, is it not the communion of the body of Christ?"
I Corinthians 11:25
"After the same manner also [he took] the cup, when he had supped, saying, This cup is the new testament in my blood: this do ye, as oft as ye drink [it], in remembrance of me."
I Thessalonians 5:10
"Who died for us, that, whether we wake or sleep, we should live together with him."
Ephesians 1:7
"In whom we have redemption through his blood, the forgiveness of sins, according to the riches of his grace."
Ephesians 2:13
"But now in Christ Jesus ye who sometimes were far off are made nigh by the blood of Christ."
Colossians 1:20
"And, having made peace through the blood of his cross, by him to reconcile all things unto himself; by him, [I say], whether [they be] things in earth, or things in heaven."
Hebrews 2:14
"Forasmuch then as the children are partakers of flesh and blood, he also himself likewise took part of the same; that through death he might destroy him that had the power of death, that is the devil."
Hebrews 9:12
"Neither by the blood of goats and calves, but by his own blood he entered in once into the holy

place, having obtained eternal redemption [for us]."

Hebrews 9:14

"How much more shall the blood of Christ, who through the eternal Spirit offered himself without spot to God, purge your conscience from dead works to serve the living God?"

Hebrews 9:28

"So Christ was once offered to bear the sins of many; and unto them that look for him shall he appear the second time without sin unto salvation."

Hebrews 10:10

"By the which will we are sanctified through the offering of the body of Jesus Christ once [for all]."

Hebrews 10:14

"For by one offering he hath perfected for ever them that are sanctified."

Hebrews 10:19

"Having therefore, brethren, boldness to enter into the holiest by the blood of Jesus."

Hebrews 12:24

"And to Jesus the mediator of the new covenant, and to the blood of sprinkling, that speaketh better things..."

I Peter 1:2

"Elect according to the foreknowledge of God the Father, through sanctification of the Spirit, unto obedience and sprinkling of the blood of Jesus Christ: Grace unto you, and peace, be multiplied."

I John 1:7

"But if we walk in the light, as he is in the light, we have fellowship one with another, and the blood of Jesus Christ his Son cleanseth us from all sin."

I John 5:8

"And there are three that bear witness in earth, the spirit, and water, and the blood: and these three agree in one."

Revelation 1:5

"And from Jesus Christ, [who is] the faithful witness, [and] the first begotten of the dead, and the prince of the kings of the earth. Unto him that loved us, and washed us from our sins in his own blood."

Conceive a Child

Genesis 17:16
"And I will bless her, and give thee a son also of her: yea, I will bless her, and she shall be [a mother] of nations; kings of people shall be of her."

Genesis 21:2
"For Sarah conceived, and bare Abraham a son in his old age, at the set time of which God had spoken to him."

Genesis 25:21
"And Isaac intreated the LORD for his wife, because she [was] barren: and the LORD was intreated of him, and Rebekah his wife conceived."

Genesis 33:5
"And he lifted up his eyes, and saw the women and children; and said, Who [are] those with thee? And he said, The children which God hath graciously given thy servant."

Exodus 23:26
"There shall nothing cast (miscarriage) their young, nor be barren, in thy land..."

Deuteronomy 7:14
"Thou shalt be blessed above all people: there shall not be male or female barren among you..."

I Samuel 1:11
"... Remember me, and not forget thine handmaid, but wilt give unto thine handmaid a man child..."

I Samuel 1:20
"Wherefore it came to pass, when the time was come about after Hannah had conceived, that she bare a son, and called his name Samuel, [saying], Because I have asked him of the LORD."

I Samuel 1:27

"For this child I prayed; and the LORD hath given me my petition which I asked of him."
I Samuel 2:20; 21
"... The LORD give thee seed of this woman.... And the LORD visited Hannah, so that she conceived, and bare three sons and two daughters...."
Judges 13:7
"...Behold, thou shalt conceive, and bear a son; now drink no wine or strong drink..."
Deuteronomy 28:11
"And the LORD shall make thee plenteous in goods, in the fruit of thy body..."
Isaiah 44:3-4
"...I will pour my spirit upon thy seed, and my blessing upon thine offspring...And they shall spring up [as] the grass, as willows by the water courses."
Isaiah 61:9
"And their seed shall be known among the Gentiles, and their offspring among the people: all that see them shall acknowledge them, that they [are] the seed [which] the LORD hath blessed."
Isaiah 65:23
"They shall not labour in vain, nor bring forth for trouble; for they [are] the seed of the blessed of the LORD, and their offspring with them."
Luke 1:36-37
"And, behold, thy cousin Elisabeth, she hath also conceived a son in her old age: and this is the sixth month with her, who was called barren. For with God nothing shall be impossible."
Romans 9:9-10
"For this [is] the word of promise, At this time will I come, and Sarah shall have a son. And not only

[this]; but when Rebecca also had conceived by one, [even] by our father Isaac."

Hebrews 11:11

"Through faith also Sarah herself received strength to conceive seed, and was delivered of a child when she was past age, because she judged him faithful who had promised."

Psalm 128:3

"Thy wife [shall be] as a fruitful vine by the sides of thine house: thy children like olive plants round about thy table."

Debt Free

Romans 13:8
"Owe no man anything, but to love one another..."
Deuteronomy 28:12
"...Thou shalt lend unto many nations, and thou shalt not borrow."
Philippians 4:19
"But my God shall supply all your need according to his riches in glory by Christ Jesus."
Romans 8:17
"And if children, then heirs; heirs of God, and joint heirs with Christ..."
II Corinthians 9:8
"And God [is] able to make all grace abound toward you; that ye, always having all sufficiency in all [things], may abound to every good work."
Genesis 14:23
"... I will not take any thing that [is] thine, lest thou shouldest say, I have made Abram rich."
Proverbs 10:22
"The blessing of the LORD, it maketh rich, and he addeth no sorrow with it."
Galatians 3:11
"...The just shall live by faith."
Matthew 6:33
"But seek ye first the kingdom of God, and his righteousness; and all these things shall be added unto you."
Matthew 18:27
"Then the lord of that servant was moved with compassion, and loosed him (released him), and forgave him the debt."
Luke 7:42

"And when they had nothing to pay, he frankly forgave them both…"

Deuteronomy 8:18

"But thou shalt remember the LORD thy God: for [it is] he that giveth thee power to get wealth, that he may establish his covenant…"

Isaiah 55:2

"Wherefore do ye spend money for [that which is] not bread? and your labour for [that which] satisfieth not?"

Proverbs 22:26-27

"Be not thou…of them that are sureties (collateral) for debts. If thou hast nothing to pay, why should he take away thy bed from under thee?"

II Kings 4:7

"Then she came and told the man of God. And he said, Go, sell the oil, and pay thy debt, and live thou and thy children of the rest."

Psalm 112:5

"A good man sheweth favour, and lendeth: he will guide his affairs with discretion."

Psalm118:8

"[It is] better to trust in the LORD than to put confidence in man."

Isaiah 57:13

"…He that putteth his trust in me shall possess the land…"

Joshua 1:8

"This book of the law shall not depart out of thy mouth; but thou shalt meditate therein day and night, that thou mayest observe to do according to all that is written therein: for then thou shalt make thy way prosperous, and then thou shalt have good success."

Deliverance from Depression

Psalm 24:7
"Lift up your heads, O ye gates; and be ye lift up, ye everlasting doors; and the King of glory shall come in."
Psalm 110:7
"He shall drink of the brook in the way: therefore shall he lift up the head."
Isaiah 29:19
"The meek also shall increase [their] joy in the LORD, and the poor among men shall rejoice in the Holy One of Israel."
Jeremiah 15:16
"Thy words were found, and I did eat them; and thy word was unto me the joy and rejoicing of mine heart..."
Ecclesiastes 9:7
"Go thy way, eat thy bread with joy..."
Psalm 5:11
"But let all those that put their trust in thee rejoice: let them ever shout for joy, because thou defendest them: let them also that love thy name be joyful in thee."
Psalm 30:5
".... Weeping may endure for a night, but joy [cometh] in the morning."
Isaiah 51:11
"...They shall obtain gladness and joy; [and] sorrow and mourning shall flee away."
Nehemiah 8:10
"...Neither be ye sorry; for the joy of the LORD is your strength."
Isaiah 53:4-5

"Surely he hath borne our griefs, and carried our sorrows….The chastisement of our peace [was] upon him; and with his stripes we are healed."
Psalm 34:1
"I will bless the LORD at all times: his praise [shall] continually [be] in my mouth."
Isaiah 26:3
"Thou wilt keep [him] in perfect peace, [whose] mind [is] stayed [on thee]: because he trusteth in thee."
Isaiah 35:10
"And the ransomed of the LORD shall return, and come to Zion with songs and everlasting joy upon their heads: they shall obtain joy and gladness, and sorrow and sighing shall flee away."
Psalm 107:20
"He sent his word, and healed them, and delivered [them] from their destructions."
I Peter 2:24
"Who his own self bare our sins in his own body on the tree, that we, being dead to sins, should live unto righteousness: by whose stripes ye were healed."
II Corinthians 10:3-5
"For though we walk in the flesh, we do not war after the flesh: (For the weapons of our warfare [are] not carnal, but mighty through God to the pulling down of strong holds;) Casting down imaginations, and every high thing that exalteth itself against the knowledge of God, and bringing into captivity every thought to the obedience of Christ."
Psalm 116:9

"I will walk before the LORD in the land of the living."

Psalm 118:17

"I shall not die, but live, and declare the works of the LORD."

Psalm 27:5

"For in the time of trouble he shall hide me in his pavilion: in the secret of his tabernacle shall he hide me; he shall set me up upon a rock."

Psalm 28:7

"The LORD [is] my strength and my shield; my heart trusted in him, and I am helped: therefore my heart greatly rejoiceth; and with my song will I praise him."

Psalm 29:11

"The LORD will give strength unto his people; the LORD will bless his people with peace."

Psalm 122:7-8

"Peace be within thy walls, [and] prosperity within thy palaces. For my brethren and companions' sakes, I will now say, Peace [be] within thee."

Psalm 32:7

"Thou [art] my hiding place; thou shalt preserve me from trouble; thou shalt compass (surround) me about with songs of deliverance."

Deliverance from Effects of Sexual Abuse

Ezekiel 16:6
"And when I passed by thee, and saw thee polluted in thine own blood, I said unto thee... Live..."
Ezekiel 16:8-9
"....I spread my skirt over thee, and covered thy nakedness...Then I washed thee with water; yea, I thoroughly washed away thy blood from thee, and I anointed thee with oil."
Psalm 34:4-5
"I sought the LORD, and he heard me, and delivered me from all my fears. They looked unto him, and were lightened: and their faces were not ashamed."
Isaiah 30:26
"... In the day that the LORD bindeth up the breach of his people, and healeth the stroke of their wound."
Jeremiah 30:17
"For I will restore health unto thee, and I will heal thee of thy wounds, saith the LORD; because they called thee an Outcast, [saying], This [is] Zion, whom no man seeketh after."
Ephesians 5:26
"That he might sanctify and cleanse it with the washing of water by the word."
Hebrews 10:22
"....our bodies washed with pure water."
Isaiah 61:3
"To appoint unto them that mourn in Zion, to give unto them beauty for ashes, the oil of joy for mourning, the garment of praise for the spirit of heaviness; that they might be called trees of

righteousness, the planting of the LORD, that he might be glorified."

Isaiah 60:18

"Violence shall no more be heard in thy land, wasting nor destruction within thy borders; but thou shalt call thy walls Salvation, and thy gates Praise."

Isaiah 41:13

"For the LORD thy God will hold thy right hand, saying unto thee, Fear not; I will help thee."

Ephesians 4:23-24

"And be renewed in the spirit of your mind; And that ye put on the new man, which after God is created in righteousness and true holiness."

Psalm 6:3-4

"My soul is also sore vexed...O LORD, deliver my soul: oh save me for thy mercies' sake."

Ezekiel 34:16

"...And will bind up [that which was] broken, and will strengthen that which was sick..."

Joel 3:10

"...Let the weak say, I [am] strong."

Matthew 25:36

"Naked, and ye clothes me..."

Revelation 21:5

"And he that sat upon the throne said, Behold, I make all things new. And he said unto me, Write: for these words are true and faithful."

Isaiah 42:3

"A bruised reed shall he not break, and the smoking flax shall he not quench: he shall bring forth judgment unto truth."

Job 11:16

"Because thou shalt forget [thy] misery, [and] remember [it] as waters [that] pass away."
Isaiah 54:4
"Fear not: for thou shalt not be ashamed: neither be thou confounded; for thou shalt not be put to shame: for thou shalt forget the shame of thy youth, and shalt not remember the reproach of thy widowhood any more."

Deliverance from Fear

Isaiah 54:4
"Fear not; for thou shalt not be ashamed: neither be thou confounded (disgraced); for thou shalt not be put to shame: for thou shalt forget the shame of thy youth, and shalt not remember the reproach of thy widowhood any more."

Isaiah 54:14
"In righteousness shalt thou be established: thou shalt be far from oppression; for thou shalt not fear: and from terror; for it shall not come near thee."

Isaiah 51:12-13
"I, [even] I, [am] he that comforteth you: who [art] thou, that thou shouldest be afraid of a man [that] shall die, and of the son of man [which] shall be made [as] grass; And forgettest the LORD thy maker, that hath stretched forth the heavens, and laid the foundations of the earth; and hast feared continually every day because of the fury of the oppressor, as if he were ready to destroy? and where [is] the fury of the oppressor?"

Deuteronomy 7:21
"Thou shalt not be affrighted at them: for the LORD thy God [is] among you, a mighty God and terrible (awesome)."

Joshua 1:9
"Have not I commanded thee? Be strong and of a good courage; be not afraid, neither be thou dismayed: for the LORD thy God [is] with thee whithersoever thou goest."

Genesis 15:1

"After these things the word of the LORD came unto Abram in a vision, saying, Fear not, Abram: I [am] thy shield, [and] thy exceeding great reward."
Isaiah 31:3
"Now the Egyptians [are] men, and not God; and their horses flesh, and not spirit. When the LORD shall stretch out his hand, both he that helpeth shall fall, and he that holpen shall fall down, and they all shall fall together."
Isaiah 35:4
"Say to them [that are] of a fearful heart, Be strong, fear not: behold, your God will come [with] vengeance, [even] God [with] a recompence; he will come and save you."
Numbers 14:9
"Only rebel not ye against the LORD, neither fear ye the people of the land; for they [are] bread for us: their defence is departed from them, and the LORD [is] with us: fear them not."
II Chronicles 20:15; 17
"...Thus saith the LORD unto you, Be not afraid nor dismayed by reason of this great multitude; for the battle [is] not yours, but God's. Ye shall not [need] to fight in this [battle]: set yourselves, stand ye [still], and see the salvation of the LORD with you..."
Psalm 27:1-2
"THE LORD [is] my light and my salvation; whom shall I fear? the LORD [is] the strength of my life; of whom shall I be afraid? When the wicked, [even] mine enemies and my foes, came upon me to eat up my flesh, they stumbled and fell."
Psalm 56:4

"In God I will praise his word, in God I have put my trust; I will not fear what flesh can do unto me."
Psalm 56:9
"When I cry [unto thee], then shall mine enemies turn back: this I know; for God [is] for me."
Psalm 56:11
"In God have I put my trust: I will not be afraid what man can do unto me."
Psalm 118:6
"The LORD [is] on my side; I will not fear: what can man do unto me?"
Matthew 6:31-32
"Therefore take no thought, saying, What shall we eat? or, What shall we drink? or, Wherewithal shall we be clothes? ... For your heavenly Father knoweth that ye have need of all these things."
Matthew 6:33
"But seek ye first the kingdom of God, and his righteousness; and all these things shall be added unto you."
Mark 4:40
"And he (Jesus) said unto them (the disciples), Why are ye so fearful? how is it that ye have no faith?"
Mark 5:34
"And he (Jesus) said unto her, Daughter, thy faith hath made thee whole; go in peace, and be whole of thy plague."
Luke 1:13
"But the angel said unto him, Fear not, Zacharias: for thy prayer is heard..."
Luke 2:10
"And the angel said unto them, Fear not: for, behold, I bring you good tidings of great joy, which shall be to all people."

Luke 8:50
"But when Jesus heard [it], he answered him, saying, Fear not: believe only, and she shall be made whole."

John 6:20
"But he (Jesus) saith unto them, It is I; be not afraid."

Acts 4:29-30
"And now, Lord, behold their threatenings: and grant unto thy servants, that with all boldness they may speak thy word, By stretching forth thine hand to heal; and that signs and wonders may be done by the name of thy holy child Jesus."

Acts 18:9-10
"Then spake the Lord to Paul in the night by a vision, Be not afraid, but speak, and hold not thy peace: For I am with thee, and no man shall set on thee to hurt thee: for I have much people in this city."

Acts 27:24
"Saying, Fear not, Paul; thou must be brought before Caesar: and, lo, God hath given thee all them that sail with thee."

Romans 8:31-32
"What shall we then say to these things? If God [be] for us, who [can be] against us? He that spared not his own Son, but delivered him up for us all, how shall he not with him also freely give us all things?"

Hebrews 13:6
"So that we may boldly say, The Lord [is] my helper, and I will not fear what man shall (can) do unto me."

II Timothy 1:7

"For God hath not given us the spirit of fear; but of power, and of love, and of a sound mind."

Deliverance from Grief

Luke 18:1
"And he (Jesus) spake a parable unto them [to this end], that men ought always to pray, and not faint (lose heart)."
Psalm 34:18
"The LORD [is] nigh unto them that are of a broken heart; and saveth such as be of a contrite (crushed) spirit."
Deuteronomy 26:14
"I have not eaten thereof in my mourning..."
Proverbs 15:13
"A merry heart maketh a cheerful countenance: but by sorrow of the heart the spirit is broken."
Proverbs 4:23
"Keep thy heart with all diligence; for out of it [are] the issues of life."
Psalm 31:9
"Have mercy upon me, O LORD, for I am in trouble: mine eye is consumed with grief, [yea], my soul and my belly."
Isaiah 14:3
"And it shall come to pass in the day that the LORD shall give thee rest from thy sorrow, and from thy fear, and from the hard bondage wherein thou wast made to serve."
John 14:1; 18
"Let not your heart be troubled: ye believe in God, believe also in me." I will not leave you comfortless: I will come to you."
II Corinthians 1:3-4
"Blessed [be] God, even the Father of our Lord Jesus Christ, the Father of mercies, and the God of

all comfort; Who comforteth us in all our tribulation, that we may be able to comfort them which are in any trouble, by the comfort wherewith we ourselves are comforted of God."

Romans 1:12

"That is, that I may be comforted together with you by the mutual faith both of you and me."

Isaiah 35:10

"And the ransomed of the LORD shall return, and come to Zion with songs and everlasting joy upon their heads: they shall obtain joy and gladness, and sorrow and sighing shall flee away."

I Thessalonians 4:13-14

"But I would not have you to be ignorant, brethren, concerning them which are asleep, that ye sorrow not, even as others which have no hope. For if we believe that Jesus died and rose again, even so them also which sleep in Jesus will God bring with him."

I Thessalonians 5:10-11

"Who died for us, that, whether we wake or sleep, we should live together with him. Wherefore comfort yourselves together, and edify one another, even as also ye do."

I Corinthians 15:51- 52

"Behold, I shew you a mystery; We shall not all sleep, but we shall all be changed, In a Moment, in the twinkling of an eye, at the last trump: for the trumpet shall sound, and the dead shall be raised incorruptible, and we shall be changed."

Matthew 11:28-30

"Come unto me, all [ye] that labour and are heavy laden, and I will give you rest. Take my yoke upon you, and learn of me; for I am meek and lowly in heart: and ye shall find rest unto your souls. For my yoke [is] easy, and my burden is light."

Deliverance from Lack

II Corinthians 8:9
"For you know the grace of our Lord Jesus Christ, that, though he was rich, yet for your sakes he became poor, that ye through his poverty might be rich."

Proverbs 10:22
"The blessing of the LORD, it maketh rich, and he addeth no sorrow with it."

Psalm 113:7-8
"He raiseth up the poor out of the dust, [and] lifteth the needy out of the dunghill; That he may set [him] with princes, [even] with princes of his people."

Ecclesiastes 5:19
"Every man also to whom God hath given riches and wealth, and hath given him power to eat thereof, and to take his portion, and to rejoice in his labour; this [is] the gift of God."

Deuteronomy 2:7
"For the LORD thy God hath blessed thee in all the works of thy hand: he knoweth thy walking through this great wilderness: these forty years the LORD thy God [hath been] with thee; thou hast lacked nothing."

Deuteronomy 8:9
"A land wherein thou shalt eat bread without scarceness, thou shalt not lack any [thing] in it…"

Psalm 23:1
"THE LORD [is] my shepherd; I shall not want."

Psalm 34:10
"…They that seek the LORD shall not want (lack) any good [thing]."

Proverbs 28:27

"He that giveth unto the poor shall not lack..."

Genesis 42:28

"And he said unto his brethren, My money is restored..."

Genesis 43:23

"And he said, Peace [be] to you, fear not: your God, and the God of your father, hath given you treasure in your sacks..."

II Corinthians 9:11

"Being enriched in every thing to all bountifulness, which causeth through us thanksgiving to God."

I Timothy 6:17

"...Nor trust in uncertain riches, but in the living God, who giveth us richly all things to enjoy."

Psalm 112:3

"Wealth and riches [shall be] in his house: and his righteousness endureth for ever."

Psalm 115:14

"The LORD shall increase you more and more, you and your children."

James 1:4

"But let patience have [her] perfect work, that ye may be perfect and entire, wanting nothing."

Psalm 37:4-5

"Delight thyself also in the LORD; and he shall give thee the desires of thine heart. Commit thy way unto the LORD; trust also in him; and he shall bring [it] to pass."

Luke 6:38

"Give, and it shall be given unto you; good measure, pressed down, and shaken together, and running over, shall men give into your bosom. For with the same measure that ye mete withal it shall be measured to you again."

Galatians 6:7; 9

"Be not deceived; God is not mocked: for whatsoever a man soweth, that shall he also reap. And let us not be weary in well doing: for in due season we shall reap, if we faint not."

Ephesians 1:3

"Blessed [be] the God and Father of our Lord Jesus Christ, who hath blessed us with all spiritual blessings in heavenly [places] in Christ."

Joshua 1:8

"This book of the law shall not depart out of thy mouth; but thou shalt mediate therein day and night, that thou mayest observe to do according to all that is written therein: for then thou shalt make thy way prosperous, and then thou shalt have good success."

III John 1:2

"Beloved, I wish above all things that thou mayest prosper and be in health, even as thy soul prospereth."

Isaiah 48:17

"...I [am] the LORD thy God which teacheth thee to profit, which leadeth thee by the way [that] thou shouldest go."

Philippians 4:19

"But my God shall supply all your need according to his riches in glory by Christ Jesus."

II Corinthians 9:8

"And God [is] able to make all grace abound toward you; that ye, always having all sufficiency in all [things], may abound to every good work."

I Thessalonians 4:12

"That ye may walk honestly toward them that are without, and [that] ye may have lack of nothing."
<u>I Thessalonians 5:23-24</u>
"And the very God of peace sanctify you wholly (completely); and [I pray God] your whole spirit and soul and body be preserved blameless unto the coming of our Lord Jesus Christ. Faithful [is] he that calleth you, who also will do [it]."

Encourage Eating

I Corinthians 10:31
"Whether therefore ye eat, or drink, or whatsoever ye do, do all to the glory of God."
Psalm 103:5
"Who satisfieth thy mouth with good [things]..."
Nehemiah 8:10
"Then he said unto them, Go your way, eat the fat, and drink the sweet, and send portions unto them for whom nothing is prepared: for [this] day [is] holy unto our Lord: neither be ye sorry; for the joy of the LORD is your strength."
Psalm 107:18-19
"Their soul abhorreth all manner of meat; and they draw near unto the gates of death. Then they cry unto the LORD in their trouble, [and] he saveth them out of their distresses."
Acts 27:34-36
"Wherefore I pray you to take [some] meat: for this is for your health: for there shall not an hair fall from the head of any of you. And when he had thus spoken, he took bread, and gave thanks to God in presence of them all: and when he had broken it, he began to eat. Then were they all of good cheer, and they also took [some] meat."
Psalm 34:8
"O taste and see that the LORD [is] good: blessed [is] the man [that] trusteth in him."
Psalm 119:103
"How sweet are thy words unto my taste! [yea, sweeter] than honey to my mouth."
Ecclesiastes 3:13

"And also that every man should eat and drink, and enjoy the good of all his labour, it [is] the gift of God."

Mark 5:43

"... And (Jesus) commanded that something should be given her to eat."

Deuteronomy 12:7

"And there ye shall eat before the LORD your God, and ye shall rejoice in all that ye put your hand unto, ye and your households, wherein the LORD thy God hath blessed thee."

Matthew 4:4

"But he answered and said, It is written, Man shall not live by bread alone, but by every word that proceedeth out of the mouth of God."

Matthew 6:11

"Give us this day our daily bread."

Isaiah 33:16

"...Bread shall be given him..."

Isaiah 55:2

"...Hearken diligently unto me, and eat ye [that which is] good, and let your soul delight itself in fatness (abundance)."

Ecclesiastes 9:7

"Go thy way, eat thy bread with joy, and drink thy wine with a merry heart; for God now accepteth thy works."

Ecclesiastes 8:15

"Then I commended mirth, because a man hath no better thing under the sun, then to eat, and to drink, and to be merry: for that shall abide with him of his labour the days of his life, which God giveth him under the sun."

Deuteronomy 8:10

"When thou hast eaten and art full, then thou shalt bless the LORD thy God for the good land which he hath given thee."

Acts 14:17

"... Filling our hearts with food and gladness."

Acts 16:34

"And when he had brought them into his house, he set meat before them, and rejoiced, believing in God with all his house."

Acts 9:19

"And when he had received meat (food) he was strengthened..."

I Chronicles 29:22

"And did eat and drink before the LORD on that day with great gladness..."

I Kings 19:5

"...Then an angel touched him, and said unto him, Arise [and] eat."

Ecclesiastes 2:24-25

"[There is] nothing better for a man, [than] that he should eat and drink, and [that] he should make his soul enjoy good in his labour. This also I saw, that it [was] from the hand of God. For who can eat, or who else can hasten (have enjoyment) [hereunto], more than I?"

Exodus 23:25

"And ye shall serve the LORD God, and he shall bless thy bread, and thy water; and I will take sickness away from the midst of thee."

Ecclesiastes 5:18

"Behold [that] which I have seen: [it is] good and comely [for one] to eat and to drink, and to enjoy the good of all his labour that he taketh under the

sun all the days of his life, which God giveth him: for it [is] his portion."
Ecclesiastes 5:19
"Every man also to whom God hath given riches and wealth, and hath given him power to eat thereof, and to take his portion, and to rejoice in his labour; this [is] the gift of God."
John 21:12
"Jesus saith unto them, Come [and] dine…"

Faith

Habakkuk 2:4
"Behold, his soul [which] is lifteth up is not upright in him: but the just shall live by his faith."
Romans 3:27
"Where [is] boasting then? It is excluded. By what law? of works? Nay: but by the law of faith."
Romans 5:1-2
"THEREFORE being justified by faith, we have peace with God through our Lord Jesus Christ: By whom also we have access by faith into this grace wherein we stand, and rejoice in hope of the glory of God."
Ephesians 2:8
"For by grace are ye saved through faith; and that not of yourselves: [it is] the gift of God."
Galatians 3:9
"So then they which be of faith are blessed with faithful Abraham."
Ephesians 6:16
"Above all, taking the shield of faith, wherewith ye shall be able to quench all the fiery darts of the wicked (wicked one)."
I Timothy 6:12
"Fight the good fight of faith, lay hold on eternal life, whereunto thou art also called, and hast professed (confessed) a good profession before many witnesses."
Hebrews 10:23
"Let us hold fast the profession of [our] faith without wavering; (for he [is] faithful that promised)."
Hebrews 11:6

"But without faith [it is] impossible to please [him]: for he that cometh to God must believe that he is, and [that] he is a rewarder of them that diligently seek him."

Romans 12:3

"...According as God hath dealt to every man the measure of faith."

Romans 10:17

"So then faith [cometh] by hearing, and hearing by the word of God."

Hebrews 6:12

"...Through faith and patience inherit the promises."

Hebrews 10:38

"Now the just shall live by faith..."

Hebrews 11:1; 3

"NOW faith is the substance of things hoped for, the evidence of things not seen. Through faith we understand that the worlds were framed by the word of God, so that things which are seen were not made of things which do appear."

Matthew 17:20

"And Jesus said unto them...If ye have faith as a grain of mustard seed, ye shall say unto this mountain, Remove hence to yonder place; and it shall remove; and nothing shall be impossible unto you."

II Corinthians 5:7

"(For we walk by faith, not by sight)."

James 1:6

"But let him ask in faith, nothing wavering..."

Galatians 5:6

"...But faith which worketh by love."

Matthew 8:13

"And Jesus said unto the centurion, Go thy way; and as thou hast believed, [so] be it done unto thee. And his servant was healed in the selfsame hour."

Matthew 9:29

"Then touched he their eyes, saying, According to your faith be it unto you."

Mark 2:5

"When Jesus saw their faith, he said unto the sick of the palsy, Son, thy sins be forgiven thee."

Acts 14:9

"The same heard Paul speak: who stedfastly beholding him, and perceiving that he had faith to be healed."

Romans 10:6

"But the righteousness which is of faith speaketh on this wise...."

Mark 9:23-24

"Jesus said unto him, If thou canst believe, all things [are] possible to him that believeth. And straightway the father of the child cried out, and said with tears, Lord, I believe; help thou mine unbelief."

Mark 11:22-24

"And Jesus answering saith unto them, Have faith in God. For verily I say unto you, That whosoever shall say unto this mountain, Be thou removed, and be thou cast into the sea; and shall not doubt in his heart, but shall believe that those things which he saith shall come to pass; he shall have whatsoever he saith. Therefore I say unto you, What things soever ye desire, when ye pray, believe that ye receive [them] and ye shall have [them]."

Forgive

Matthew 5:23-24
"Therefore if thou bring thy gift to the altar, and there rememberest that thy brother hath ought against thee; Leave there thy gift before the altar, and go thy way; first be reconciled to thy brother, and then come and offer thy gift."
Matthew 6:12
"And forgive us our debts, as we forgive our debtors."
Matthew 7:12
"Therefore all things whatsoever ye would that men should do to you, do ye even so to them…"
Matthew 18:15
"Moveover if thy brother shall trespass against thee, go and tell him his fault between thee and him alone: if he shall hear thee, thou hast gained thy brother."
Matthew 18:21-22
"Then came Peter to him, and said, Lord, how oft shall my brother sin against me, and I forgive him? till seven times? Jesus saith unto him, I say not unto thee, Until seven times: but, Until seventy times seven."
Matthew 18:32-33
"…I forgave thee all that debt, because thou desiredst me: Shouldest not thou also have had compassion on thy fellowservant, even as I had pity on thee?"
Mark 11:25
"And when you stand praying, forgive, if you have ought against any: that your Father also which is in heaven may forgive you your trespasses."

Luke 7:41-42

"There was a certain creditor which had two debtors: the one owed five hundred pence, and the other fifty. And when they had nothing to pay, he frankly forgave them both. Tell me therefore, which of them will love him most?"

Luke 17:3-4

"Take heed to yourselves: If thy brother trespass against thee, rebuke him; and if he repent, forgive him. And if he trespass against thee seven times in a day, and seven times in a day turn again to thee, saying, I repent; thou shalt forgive him."

John 20:23

"Whose soever sins ye remit, they are remitted unto them..."

II Corinthians 2:7

"So that contrariwise ye [ought] rather to forgive [him], and comfort [him], lest perhaps such a one should be swallowed up with overmuch sorrow."

II Corinthians 2:10-11

"To whom ye forgive any thing, I [forgive] also: for if I forgave any thing, to whom I forgave [it], for your sakes [forgave I it] in the person (presence) of Christ. Lest Satan should get an advantage of us: for we are not ignorant of his devices."

Job 42:10

"And the LORD turned the captivity of Job, when he prayed for his friends: also the LORD gave Job twice as much as he had before."

Philippians 2:14-15

"Do all things without murmurings and disputings. That ye may be blameless and harmless, the sons of God, without rebuke, in the midst of a crooked and perverse nation, among whom ye shine as lights in the world."

Ephesians 4:32

"And be ye kind one to another, tenderhearted, forgiving one another, even as God for Christ's sake hath forgiven you."

Romans 12:14

"Bless them which persecute you: bless, and curse not."

Romans 12:17

"Recompense to no man evil for evil. Provide things honest in the sight of all men."

Romans 12:19

"Dearly beloved, avenge not yourselves... for it is written, Vengeance [is] mine; I will repay, saith the LORD."

Romans 12:20-21

"Therefore if thine enemy hunger, feed him; if he thirst, give him drink... Be not overcome of evil, but overcome evil with good."

Colossians 3:23

"And whatsoever ye do, do [it] heartily, as to the Lord, and not unto men."

Colossians 3:24

"Knowing that of the Lord ye shall receive the reward of the inheritance: for ye serve the Lord Christ."

Colossians 3:25

"But he that doeth wrong shall receive for the wrong which he hath done: and there is no respect of persons."

God's Promises About Children

Jeremiah 31:16-17
"Thus saith the LORD; Refrain thy voice from
weeping, and thine eyes from tears: for thy work
shall be rewarded, saith the LORD; and they
(children) shall come again from the land of the
enemy. And there is hope in thine end, saith the
LORD, that thy children shall come again to their
own border."

Isaiah 49:25
"...I will contend with him that contendeth with
thee, and I will save thy children."

Psalm 145:9
"The LORD [is] good to all: and his tender mercies
[are] over all his works."

Genesis 18:19
"For I know him, that he will command his children
and his household after him, and they shall keep
the way of the LORD, to do justice and judgment;
that the LORD may bring upon Abraham that which
he hath spoken of him."

Proverbs 22:6
"Train up a child in the way he should go: and
when he is old, he shall not depart from it."

Acts 20:32
"And now, brethren, I commend you to God, and to
the word of his grace, which is able to build you up,
and to give you an inheritance among all them
which are sanctified."

Deuteronomy 6:6-7
"And these words, which I command thee this day,
shall be in thine heart: And thou shalt teach them
diligently unto thy children, and shalt talk of them

when thou sittest in thine house, and when thou walkest by the way, and when thou liest down, and when thou riseth up."

Deuteronomy 7:13-14

"And he will love thee, and bless thee, and multiply thee: he will also bless the fruit of thy womb.... Thou shalt be blessed above all people: there shall not male or female barren among you..."

Isaiah 44:3

"... I will pour my spirit upon thy seed, and my blessing upon thine offspring."

Isaiah 59:21

"As for me, this [is] my covenant with them, saith the LORD; My spirit that [is] upon thee, and my words which I have put in thy mouth, shall not depart out of thy mouth, nor out of the mouth of thy seed, nor out of the mouth of thy seed's seed, saith the LORD, from henceforth and for ever."

Psalm 112:1-2

"PRAISE ye the LORD. Blessed [is] the man [that] feareth (reverence) the LORD, [that] delighteth greatly in his commandments. His seed shall be mighty upon earth: the generation of the upright shall be blessed."

Deuteronomy 11:19

"And ye shall teach them your children, speaking of them when thou sittest in thine house, and when thou walkest by the way, when thou liest down, and when thou risest up."

Psalm 115:14-15

"The LORD shall increase you more and more, you and your children. Ye [are] blessed of the LORD which made heaven and earth."

Psalm 144:12

"That our sons [may be] as plants grown up in their youth; [that] our daughters [may be] as corner stones, polished [after] the similitude of a palace."
Isaiah 54:13
"And all thy children [shall be] taught of the LORD; and great [shall be] the peace of thy children."
Isaiah 61:9
"And their seed shall be known among the Gentiles, and their offspring among the people: all that see them shall acknowledge them, that they [are] the seed [which] the LORD hath blessed."
Isaiah 8:18
"Behold, I and the children whom the LORD hath given me [are] for signs and for wonders in Israel from the LORD of hosts, which dwelleth in mount Zion."
Isaiah 38:19
".... The father to the children shall make known thy truth."
Acts 2:39
"For the promise is unto you, and your children, and to all that are afar off, [even] as many as the Lord our God shall call."
Proverbs 11:21
"... But the seed of the righteous shall be delivered."
Proverbs 20:7
"The just [man], walketh in his integrity: his children [are] blessed after him."
Psalm 37:25
"I have been young, and [now] am old; yet have I not seen the righteous forsaken, nor his seed begging bread."
Zechariah 10:7-8

"...Yea, their children shall [see it], and be glad; their heart shall rejoice in the LORD. I will hiss for them, and gather them; for I have redeemed them: and they shall increase as they have increased."
Psalm 147:13
"...He hath blessed thy children within thee."

Grace

Genesis 39:4
"And Joseph found grace in his sight, and he served him: and made him overseer over his house, and all [that] he had he put into his hand."

Exodus 3:21
"And I will give this people favour in the sight of the Egyptians: and it shall come to pass, that, when ye go, ye shall not go empty."

Titus 2:11-12
"For the grace of God that bringeth salvation hath appeared to all men, Teaching us that, denying ungodliness and worldly lusts, we should live soberly, righteously, and godly, in this present world."

Titus 3:7
"That being justified by his grace, we should be made heirs according to the hope of eternal life."

Zechariah 4:7
"...Grace, grace unto it."

Romans 4:16
"Therefore [it is] of faith, that [it might be] by grace; to the end the promise might be sure to all the seed; not to that only which is of the law, but to that also which is of the faith of Abraham; who is the father of us all."

Romans 5:15
"But not as the offence, so also [is] the free gift. For if through the offence of one (Adam) many be dead, much more the grace of God, and the gift by grace, [which is] by one man, Jesus Christ, hath abounded unto many."

Ephesians 2:5

"Even when we were dead in sins, hath quickened us together with Christ, (by grace ye are saved)."
Ephesians 2:8
"For by grace are ye saved through faith; and that not of yourselves: [it is] the gift of God."
Luke 2:40; 52
"And the child grew, and waxed (became) strong in spirit, filled with wisdom: and the grace of God was upon him. And Jesus increased in wisdom and stature, and in favour with God and man."
II Corinthians 4:15
"For all things [are] for your sakes, that the abundant grace might through the thanksgiving of many redound to the glory of God."
II Corinthians 9:8
"And God [is] able to make all grace abound toward you; that ye, always having all sufficiency in all [things], may abound to every good work."
II Corinthians 12:9
"And he said unto me, My grace is sufficient for thee: for my strength is made perfect in weakness..."
II Peter 1:2
Grace and peace be multiplied unto you through the knowledge of God, and Jesus our Lord."
I Peter 5:5
"...For God resisteth the proud, and giveth grace to the humble."
II Timothy 2:1
"Thou therefore, my son, be strong in the grace that is in Christ Jesus."
Hebrews 4:16

"Let us therefore come boldly unto the throne of grace, that we may obtain mercy, and find grace to help in time of need."

James 4:6

"But he giveth more grace, Wherefore he saith, God resisteth the proud, but giveth grace unto the humble."

I Corinthians 15:10

"But by the grace of God I am what I am: and his grace which [was bestowed] upon me was not in vain; but I laboured more abundantly than they all: yet not I, but the grace of God which was with me."

Guidance

Isaiah 48:17
"Thus saith the LORD, thy Redeemer, the Holy One of Israel; I [am] the LORD thy God which teacheth thee to profit, which leadeth thee by the way [that] thou shouldest go."

Isaiah 30:21
 "And thine ears shall hear a word behind thee, saying, This [is] the way, walk ye in it, when ye turn to the right hand, and when ye turn to the left."

Psalm 32:8
"I will instruct thee and teach thee in the way which thou shalt go: I will guide thee with mine eye."

Psalm 73:24
"Thou shalt guide me with thy counsel, and afterward receive me [to] glory."

Isaiah 58:11
"And the LORD shall guide thee continually, and satisfy thy soul in drought, and make fat thy bones: and thou shalt be like a watered garden, and like a spring of water, whose waters fail not."

Proverbs 16:3
"Commit thy works unto the LORD, and thy thoughts shall be established."

Matthew 7:7-8
"Ask, and it shall be given you; seek, and ye shall find; knock, and it shall be opened unto you: For every one that asketh receiveth; and he that seeketh findeth; and to him that knocketh it shall be opened."

Isaiah 52:12

"For ye shall not go out with haste, nor go by flight: for the LORD will go before you; and the God of Israel [will be] your rereward."
Psalm 16:11
"Thou wilt shew me the path of life: in thy presence [is] fullness of joy; at thy right hand [there are] pleasures for evermore."
Proverbs 6:22
"When thou goest, it shall lead thee; when thou sleepest, it shall keep thee; and [when] thou awakest, it shall talk with thee."
Jeremiah 29:12-13
"Then shall ye call upon me, and ye shall go and pray unto me, and I will hearken unto you. And ye shall seek me, and find [me], when ye shall search for me with all your heart."
Matthew 6:10
"Thy kingdom come. Thy will be done in earth as [it is] in heaven."
Matthew 18:18
"Verily I say unto you, Whatsoever ye shall bind on earth shall be bound in heaven: and whatsoever ye shall loose on earth shall be loosed in heaven."
Psalm 40:8
"I delight to do thy will, O my God: yea, thy law [is] within my heart."
I Corinthians 2:10
"But God hath revealed [them] unto us by his Spirit: for the Spirit searcheth all things, yea, the deep things of God."
I Corinthians 2:16
"For who hath known the mind of the Lord, that he may instruct him? But we have the mind of Christ."
Isaiah 55:11

"So shall my word be that goeth forth out of my mouth: it shall not return unto me void, but it shall accomplish that which I please, and it shall prosper [in the thing] whereto I send it."

Genesis 24:48

"And I bowed down my head, and worshipped the LORD, and blessed the LORD God of my master Abraham, which had led me in the right way to take my master's brother's daughter unto his son."

Healing

Exodus 15:26
"...For I am the LORD that healeth thee."

Exodus 23:25
"And ye shall serve the LORD your God, and he shall bless thy bread, and thy water; and I will take sickness away from the midst of thee."

Jeremiah 30:17
"For I will restore health unto thee, and I will heal thee of thy wounds, saith the LORD; because they called thee an Outcast, [saying], This [is] Zion, whom no man seeketh after."

II Chronicles 30:20
"And the LORD hearkened unto Hezekiah, and healed the people."

Psalm 107:20
"He sent his word, and healed them, and delivered [them] from their destructions."

I Peter 2:24
"Who his own self bare our sins in his own body on the tree, that we, being dead to sins, should live unto righteousness: by whose stripes ye were healed."

Titus 2:14
"Who gave himself for us, that he might redeem us from all iniquity, and purify unto himself a peculiar people, zealous of good works."

Proverbs 4:20-22
"My son, attend to my words; incline thine ear unto my sayings. Let them not depart from thine eyes; keep them in the midst of thine heart. For they [are] life unto those that find them, and health to all their flesh."

Proverbs 3:1-2

"My son, forget not my law; but let thine heart keep my commandments: For length of days, and long life, and peace, shall they add to thee."

Proverbs 3:7-8

"Be not wise in thine own eyes: fear (honor) the LORD, and depart from evil. It shall be health to thy navel, and marrow to thy bones."

Proverbs 20:27

"The spirit of man [is] the candle of the LORD, searching all the inward parts of the belly."

Isaiah 33:24

"And the inhabitant shall not say, I am sick: the people that dwell therein [shall be] forgiven [their] iniquity."

Isaiah 53:4-5

"Surely he hath borne our griefs, and carried our sorrows: yet we did esteem him stricken, smitten of God and afflicted. But he [was] wounded for our transgressions, [he was] bruised for our iniquities: the chastisement of our peace [was] upon him; and with his stripes were are healed."

Psalm 139:16

"Thine eyes did see my substance, yet being unperfect (unformed); and in thy book all [my members] were written, [which] in continuance were fashioned, when [as yet there was] none of them."

II Kings 5:14

"Then went he down, and dipped himself seven times in the Jordan, according to the saying of the man of God: and his flesh came again like unto the flesh of a little child, and he was clean."

Proverbs 17:22

"A merry heart doeth good [like] a medicine..."
Job 33:25
"His flesh shall be fresher than a child's: he shall return to the days of his youth."
Psalm 103:2-3
"Bless the LORD, O my soul, and forget not all his benefits: Who forgiveth all thine iniquities; who healeth all thy diseases."
Psalm 116:9
"I will walk before the LORD in the land of the living."
Psalm 118:17
"I shall not die, but live, and declare the works of the LORD."
Matthew 8:8
"...Speak the word only, and my servant shall be healed."
Matthew 8:13
"And Jesus said unto the centurion, Go thy way; and as thou hast believed, [so] be it done unto thee. And his servant was healed in the selfsame hour."
Matthew 8:16-17
"...And he cast out the spirits with [his] word, and healed all that were sick: That it might be fulfilled which was spoken by Esaias the prophet, saying, Himself took our infirmities, and bare [our] sicknesses."
Matthew 9:35
"And Jesus went about all the cities and villages, teaching in their synagogues, and preaching the gospel of the kingdom, and healing every sickness and every disease among the people."
Mark 5:28; 34

"For she said, If I may touch but his clothes, I shall be whole. And he said unto her, Daughter, thy faith hath made the whole; go in peace, and be whole of thy plague."

Mark 5:41

"...Damsel, I say unto thee, arise."

Luke 5:12-13

"...Saying, Lord, if thou wilt, thou canst make me clean. And he (Jesus) put forth [his] hand, and touched him, saying, I will: be thou clean. And immediately the leprosy departed from him."

Acts 3:6; 16

"...In the name of Jesus Christ of Nazareth rise up and walk. And his name through faith in his name hath made this man strong, whom ye see and know: yea, the faith which is by him hath given him this perfect soundness in the presence of you all."

Acts 4:10

"Be it known unto you all, and to all the people of Israel, that by the name of Jesus Christ of Nazareth, whom ye crucified, whom God raised from the dead, [even] by him doth this man stand here before you whole."

Acts 4:30

"By stretching forth thine hand to heal; and that signs and wonders may be done by the name of thy holy child Jesus."

Acts 9:40

"But Peter put them all forth, and kneeled down, and prayed; and turning [him] to the body said, Tabitha, arise. And she opened her eyes: and when she saw Peter, she sat up."

James 5:13

"Is any among you afflicted? let him pray. Is any merry? let him sing psalms."
James 5:14
"Is any sick among you? let him call for the elders of the church: and let them pray over him, anointing him with oil in the name of the Lord."
James 5:15
"And the prayer of faith shall save the sick, and the Lord shall raise him up; and if he have committed sins, they shall be forgiven him."
James 5:16
"Confess [your] faults one to another, and pray one for another, that ye may be healed. The effectual fervent prayer of a righteous man availeth much."
III John 1:2
"Beloved, I wish above all things that thou mayest prosper and be in health, even as thy soul prospereth."
Nahum 1:9
"...Affliction shall not rise up the second time."
Psalm 147:3
"He healeth the broken in heart, and bindeth up their wounds."
Jeremiah 17:14
"Heal me, O LORD, and I shall be healed; save me, and I shall be saved: for thou [art] my praise."

House

Psalm 127:1
"EXCEPT the LORD build the house, they labour in vain that build it..."
Proverbs 24:3
"Through wisdom is an house builded; and by understanding it is established."
Psalm 107:7
"And he led them forth by the right way, that they might go to a city of habitation."
Psalm 16:5
"The LORD [is] the portion of mine inheritance and of my cup: thou maintainest my lot."
Hebrews 3:4
"For every house is builded by some [man]; but he that built all things [is] God."
Proverbs 12:7
"...The house of the righteous shall stand."
Psalm 18:19
" He brought me forth also into a large place..."
II Samuel 7:10; 27
"...That they may dwell in a place of their own, and move no more; neither shall the children of wickedness afflict them any more, as beforetime ...Hast revealed to thy servant, saying, I will build thee an house..."
Proverbs 3:33
"...But he blesseth the habitation of the just."
Psalm 66:12
"...But thou broughtest us out into a wealthy [place]."
Psalm 105:44

"And gave them the lands of the heathen: and they inherited the labour of the people."
Isaiah 65:21
"And they shall build houses, and inhabit [them]; and they shall plant vineyards, and eat the fruit of them."
Isaiah 54:12
"And I will make thy windows of agates, and thy gates of carbuncles, and all thy borders of pleasant stones."
Proverbs 24:4
"And by knowledge shall the chambers be filled with all precious and pleasant riches."
Psalm 112:3
"Wealth and riches [shall be] in his house: and his righteousness endureth for ever."
Proverbs 15:6
"In the house of the righteous [is] much treasure..."
Deuteronomy 6:11
"And houses full of good [things], which thou filledst not, and wells digged, which thou diggedst not, vineyards and olive trees, which thou plantedst not..."
Psalm 122:7
"Peace be within thy walls, [and] prosperity within thy palaces."
II Samuel 7:29
"Therefore now let it please thee to bless the house of thy servant, that it may continue for ever before thee: for thou, O LORD GOD, hast spoken [it]: and with thy blessing let the house of thy servant be blessed for ever."
I Chronicles 17:25

"For thou, O my God, hast told thy servant that thou wilt build him an house: therefore thy servant hath found [in his heart] to pray before thee."
II Peter 1:3
"According as his divine power hath given unto us all things that [pertain] unto life and godliness, through the knowledge of him that hath called us to glory and virtue."
Philippians 4:19
"But my God shall supply all your need according to his riches in glory by Christ Jesus."
I Timothy 6:17
"Charge them that are rich in this world, that they be not highminded, nor trust in uncertain riches, but in the living God, who giveth us richly all things to enjoy."

Joy

Isaiah 51:11
"Therefore the redeemed of the LORD shall return, and come with singing unto Zion; and everlasting joy [shall be] upon their head: they shall obtain gladness and joy; [and] sorrow and mourning shall flee away."

John 16:24
"Hitherto have ye asked nothing in my name: ask, and ye shall receive, that your joy may be full."

Nehemiah 8:10
"… Neither be ye sorry; for the joy of the LORD is your strength."

Psalm 5:11
"But let all those that put their trust in thee rejoice: let them ever shout for joy, because thou defendest them: let them also that love thy name be joyful in thee."

Ecclesiastes 5:18
"Behold [that] which I have seen: [it is] good and comely [for one] to eat and to drink, and to enjoy the good of all his labour that he taketh under the sun all the days of his life, which God giveth him: for it [is] his portion."

Isaiah 29:19
"The meek also shall increase [their] joy in the LORD, and the poor among men shall rejoice in the Holy One of Israel."

Luke 1:14
"And thou shalt have joy and gladness; and many shall rejoice at his birth."

Luke 2:10

"And the angel said unto them, Fear not: for, behold, I bring you good tidings of great joy, which shall be to all people."

Habakkuk 3:18

"Yet I will rejoice in the LORD, I will joy in the God of my salvation."

Psalm 30:5

"...In his favour [is] life: weeping may endure for a night, but joy [cometh] in the morning."

Psalm 51:12

"Restore unto me the joy of thy salvation; and uphold me [with thy] free spirit."

Psalm 126:5

"They that sow in tears shall reap in joy."

Isaiah 35:10

"And the ransomed of the LORD shall return, and come to Zion with songs and everlasting joy upon their heads: they shall obtain joy and gladness, and sorrow and sighing shall flee away."

Acts 8:8

"And there was great joy in that city."

Luke 15:7

"I say unto you, that likewise joy shall be in heaven over one sinner that repenteth..."

John 15:11

"These things have I spoken unto you, that my joy might remain in you, and [that] your joy might be full."

James 1:2-4

"My brethren, count it all joy when ye fall into divers temptations; Knowing [this], that the trying of your faith worketh patience. But let patience have [her] perfect work, that ye may be perfect (complete, mature) and entire, wanting nothing."

Philippians 1:4

"Always in every prayer of mine for you all making request with joy."

Philippians 2:2

"Fulfil ye my joy, that ye be likeminded, having the same love, [being] of one accord, of one mind."

Psalm 16:11

"Thou wilt shew me the path of life: in thy presence [is] fullness of joy; at thy right hand [there are] pleasures for ever more."

Live Long and Strong

Proverbs 3:1-2
"MY son, forget not my law; but let thine heart keep my commandments: For length of days, and long life, and peace, shall they add to thee."

Proverbs 3:13; 16
"Happy [is] the man [that] findeth wisdom, and the man [that] getteth understanding. Length of days [is] in her right hand; [and] in her left hand riches and honour."

Deuteronomy 25:15
"...That thy days may be lengthened in the land which the LORD thy God giveth thee."

Deuteronomy 34:7
"And Moses was an hundred and twenty years old when he died: his eye was not dim, nor his natural force abated."

Proverbs 4:10
"Hear, O my son, and receive my sayings; and the years of thy life shall be many."

Proverbs 4:13
"Take fast (firm) hold of instruction; let [her] not go: keep her; for she [is] thy life."

Proverbs 4:20-22
"My son, attend to my words; incline thine ear unto my sayings. Let them not depart from thine eyes; keep them in the midst of thine heart. For they [are] life unto those that find them, and health to all their flesh."

Job 42:16
"After this lived Job an hundred and forty years, and saw his sons, and his son's sons, [even] four generations."

Exodus 23:26
".... The number of thy days I will fulfill."
Psalm 91:16
"With long life will I satisfy him, and shew him my salvation."
Genesis 43:28
"...Our father [is] in good health, he [is] yet alive..."
Psalm 103:2; 5
"Bless the LORD, O my soul, and forget not all his benefits: Who satisfieth thy mouth with good [things]; [so that] thy youth is renewed like the eagle's."
Genesis 6:3
"...Yet his days shall be an hundred and twenty years."
Isaiah 46:4
"And [even] to [your] old age I [am] he; and [even] to hoar (gray) hairs will I carry [you]: I have made, and I will bear; even I will carry, and deliver [you]."
Isaiah 65:20
"There shall be no more thence an infant of days, nor an old man that hath not filled his days..."
Genesis 15:15
"And thou shalt go to thy fathers in peace; thou shalt be buried in a good old age."
Genesis 25:8
"Then Abraham gave up the ghost, and died in a good old age, an old man, and full [of years] and was gathered to his people."
Joshua 14:10-11
"And now, behold, the LORD hath kept me alive, as he said, these forty and five years, even since the LORD spake this word unto Moses...and now, lo, I [am] this day fourscore and five years old (85). As

yet I [am as] strong this day as [I was] in the day that Moses sent me: as my strength [was] then, even so [is] my strength now, for war, both to go out, and to come in."

Psalm 116:9

"I will walk before the LORD in the land of the living."

Psalm 118:17

"I shall not die, but live and declare the works of the LORD."

Job 11:17

"And [thine] age shall be clearer than the noonday; thou shalt shine forth, thou shalt be as the morning."

Love

John 3:16
"For God so loved the world, that he gave his only begotten Son, that whosoever believeth in him should not perish, but have everlasting life."
Romans 5:8
"But God commendeth his love toward us, in that, while we were yet sinners, Christ died for us."
I John 4:10
"Herein is love, not that we loved God, but that he loved us, and sent his Son [to be] the propitiation for our sins."
Titus 3:4
"But after that the kindness and love of God our Saviour toward man appeared."
Jeremiah 31:3
"The LORD hath appeared of old unto me, [saying], Yea, I have loved thee with an everlasting love: therefore with lovingkindness have I drawn thee."
Isaiah 38:17
"Behold, for peace I had great bitterness: but thou hast in love to my soul [delivered it] from the pit of corruption: for thou hast cast all my sins behind thy back."
Romans 5:5
"And hope maketh not ashamed; because the love of God is shed abroad in our hearts by the Holy Ghost which is given us."
I John 3:23
"And this is his commandment, That we should believe on the name of his Son Jesus Christ, and love one another, as he gave us commandment."
Mark 12:30-31

"And thou shalt love the Lord thy God with all thy heart, and with all thy soul, and with all thy mind, and with all thy strength: this [is] the first commandment. And the second [is] like, [namely] this, Thou shalt love thy neighbor as thyself. There is none other commandment greater than these."

John 13:34

"A new commandment I give unto you, That ye love one another; as I have loved you, that ye also love one another."

Matthew 5:44-45

"But I say unto you, Love your enemies, bless them that curse you, do good to them that hate you, and pray for them which despitefully use you, and persecute you; That ye may be the children of your Father which is in heaven: for he maketh his sun to rise on the evil and on the good, and sendeth rain on the just and on the unjust."

I John 4:19

"We love him, because he first loved us."

Psalm 18:1

"I WILL love thee, O LORD, my strength."

Psalm 31:23

"O love the LORD, all ye his saints: [for] the LORD preserveth the faithful, and plentifully rewardeth the proud doer."

Psalm 91:14

"Because he hath set his love upon me, therefore will I deliver him: I will set him on high, because he hath known my name."

Psalm 5:11

"But let all those that put their trust in thee rejoice: let them ever shout for joy, because thou

defendest them: let them also that love thy name be joyful in thee."
Psalm 116:1
"I LOVE the LORD, because he hath heard my voice [and] my supplications."
Colossians 3:14
"And above all these things [put on] charity (love), which is the bond of perfectness."
John 14:21
"He that hath my commandments, and keepeth them, he it is that loveth me: and he that loveth me shall be loved of my Father, and I will love him, and will manifest myself to him."
John 15:10
"If ye keep my commandments, ye shall abide in my love; even as I have kept my Father's commandments, and abide in his love."
Romans 8:37
"Nay, in all these things we are more than conquerors through him that loved us."
Romans 12:9-10
"[Let] love be without dissimulation. Abhor that which is evil; cleave to that which is good. [Be] kindly affectioned one to another with brotherly love; in honour preferring one another."
I John 4:16
"And we have known and believed the love that God hath to us. God is love; and he that dwelleth in love dwelleth in God, and God in him."
I John 4:17
"Herein is our love made perfect, that we may have boldness in the day of judgment: because as he is, so are we in this world."
I John 4:18

"There is no fear in love; but perfect love casteth out fear: because fear hath torment. He that feareth is not made perfect in love."

II Timothy 1:7

"For God hath not given us the spirit of fear; but of power, and of love, and of a sound mind."

I Corinthians 16:14

"Let all your things be done with charity (love)."

I Corinthians 13- The Entire Chapter- Here are a few verses

I Corinthians 13:4

"Charity (love) suffereth long, [and is] kind; charity envieth not; charity vaunteth not itself, is not puffed up."

I Corinthians 13:8

"Charity (love) never faileth..."

Peace

John 14:27
"Peace I leave with you, my peace I give unto you: not as the world giveth, give I unto you. Let not your heart be troubled, neither let it be afraid."

Colossians 3:15
"And let the peace of God rule in your hearts, to the which also ye are called in one body; and be ye thankful."

John 16:33
"These things I have spoken unto you, that in me ye might have peace. In the world ye shall have tribulation: but be of good cheer; I have overcome the world."

Romans 5:1
"THEREFORE being justified by faith, we have peace with God through our Lord Jesus Christ."

Isaiah 26:3
"Thou wilt keep [him] in perfect peace, [whose] mind [is] stayed [on thee]: because he trusteth in thee."

Romans 8:6
"For to be carnally minded [is] death; but to be spiritually minded [is] life and peace."

Philippians 4:9
"Those things, which ye have both learned, and received, and heard, and seen in me, do: and the God of peace shall be with you."

Psalm 46:1-2
"GOD is our refuge and strength, a very present help in trouble. Therefore will not we fear, though the earth be removed, and though the mountains be carried into the midst of the sea."

Psalm 46:10-11

"Be still, and know that I [am] God: I will be exalted among the heathen, I will be exalted in the earth. The LORD of hosts [is] with us; the God of Jacob [is] our refuge. Selah."

Psalm 122:7-8

"Peace be within thy walls, [and] prosperity within thy palaces. For my brethren and companions' sakes, I will now say, Peace [be] within thee."

Isaiah 30:15

"For thus saith the LORD GOD, the Holy One of Israel; In returning and rest shall ye be saved; in quietness and in confidence shall be your strength...."

Hebrews 10:35

"Cast not away therefore your confidence, which hath great recompence of reward."

Hebrews 13:5

"[Let your] conversation [be] without covetousness; [and be] content with such things as ye have: for he hath said, I will never leave thee, nor forsake thee."

Ephesians 3:12

"In whom we have boldness and access with confidence by the faith of him."

Proverbs 3:26

"For the LORD shall be thy confidence, and shall keep thy foot from being taken."

Philippians 1:6

"Being confident of this very thing, that he which hath begun a good work in you will perform [it] until the day of Jesus Christ."

I John 5:14-15

"And this is the confidence that we have in him, that, if we ask any thing according to his will, he heareth us: And if we know that he hear us, whatsoever we ask, we know that we have the petitions that we desired of him."
I John 2:28
"And now, little children, abide in him; that, when he shall appear, we may have confidence, and not be ashamed before him at his coming."

Power of Words/Tongues

Matthew 12:34
"...For out of the abundance of the heart the mouth speaketh."

Matthew 12:35
"A good man out of the good treasure of the heart bringeth forth good things: and an evil man out of the evil treasure bringeth forth evil things."

Matthew 12:37
"For by thy words thou shalt be justified, and by thy words thou shalt be condemned."

Mark 4:14
"The sower soweth the word."

Romans 10:8
"...The word is nigh thee, [even] in thy mouth, and in thy heart: that is, the word of faith, which we preach."

Proverbs 21:23
"Whoso keepeth his mouth and his tongue keepeth his soul from troubles."

Proverbs 18:4
"The words of a man's mouth [are as] deep waters, [and] the wellspring of wisdom [as] a flowing brook."

Proverbs 18:21
"Death and life [are] in the power of the tongue: and they that love it shall eat the fruit thereof."

Proverbs 15:1
"A SOFT answer turneth away wrath: but grievous words stir up anger."

Proverbs 15:2
"The tongue of the wise useth knowledge aright: but the mouth of fools poureth out foolishness."

Proverbs 15:4

"A wholesome tongue [is] a tree of life: but perverseness therein [is] a breach in the spirit."

Proverbs 15:23

"A man hath joy by the answer of his mouth: and a word [spoken] in due season, how good [is it]!"

Romans 10:10

"For with the heart man believeth unto righteousness; and with the mouth confession is made unto salvation."

Isaiah 28:11

"For with stammering lips and another tongue will he speak to this people."

I Corinthians 14:2

"For he that speaketh in an [unknown] tongue speaketh not unto men, but unto God: for no man understandeth [him]; howbeit in the spirit he speaketh mysteries."

I Corinthians 14:4

"He that speaketh in an [unknown] tongue edifieth himself..."

I Corinthians 14:13-14

"Wherefore let him that speaketh in an [unknown] tongue pray that he may interpret. For if I pray in an [unknown] tongue, my spirit prayeth, but my understanding is unfrutitful."

Acts 2:3-4

"And there appeared unto them cloven tongues like as of fire, and it sat upon each of them. And they were all filled with the Holy Ghost, and began to speak with other tongues, as the Spirit gave them utterance."

Acts 10:44

"While Peter yet spake these words, the Holy Ghost fell on all them which heard the word."
Acts 10:46-47

"For they heard them speak with tongues, and magnify God. Then answered Peter, Can any man forbid water, that these should not be baptized, which have received the Holy Ghost as well as we?"
Acts 19:6

"And when Paul had laid [his] hands upon them, the Holy Ghost came on them; and they spake with tongues, and prophesied."
I Corinthians 2:13

"Which things also we speak, not in the words which man's wisdom teacheth, but which the Holy Ghost teacheth; comparing spiritual things with spiritual."
I Corinthians 2:14

"But the natural man receiveth not the things of the Spirit of God: for they are foolishness unto him: neither can he know [them], because they are spiritually discerned."
I Corinthians 2:15-16

"But he that is spiritual judgeth all things, yet he himself is judged of no man. For who hath known the mind of the Lord, that he may instruct him? But we have the mind of Christ."
Romans 8:26

"Likewise the Spirit also helpeth our infirmities (weaknesses): for we know not what we should pray for as we ought: but the Spirit itself maketh intercession for us with groanings which cannot be uttered."
Romans 8:27-28

"And he that searcheth the hearts knoweth what [is] the mind of the Spirit, because he maketh intercession for the saints according to [the will of] God. And we know that all things work together for good to them that love God, to them who are the called according to [his] purpose."

Praise

Isaiah 63:7
"I will mention the lovingkindnesses of the LORD, [and] the praises of the LORD, according to all that the LORD hath bestowed on us, and the great goodness toward the house of Israel, which he hath bestowed on them according to his mercies, and according to the multitude of his lovingkindnesses."
Isaiah 38:19
"The living, the living, he shall praise thee, as I [do] this day..."
Colossians 1:12
"Giving thanks unto the Father, which hath made us meet to be partakers of the inheritance of the saints in light."
I Thessalonians 5:16
"Rejoice evermore."
I Thessalonians 5:18
"In every thing give thanks: for this is the will of God in Christ Jesus concerning you."
Psalm 100:4
"Enter into his gates with thanksgiving, [and] into his courts with praise: be thankful unto him, [and] bless his name."
Psalm 103:1
"BLESS the LORD, O my soul: and all that is within me, [bless] his holy name."
Psalm 107:1
"O GIVE thanks unto the LORD, for [he is] good: for his mercy [endureth] for ever."
Psalm 118:21

"I will praise thee: for thou hast heard me, and art become my salvation."
Psalm 139:14
"I will praise thee; for I am fearfully [and] wonderfully made..."
Psalms 146:1-2
"PRAISE ye the LORD. Praise the LORD, O my soul. While I live will I praise the LORD: I will sing praises unto my God while I have any being."
Psalm 147:1
"PRAISE ye the LORD: for [it is] good to sing praises unto our God; for [it is] pleasant; [and] praise is comely."
Psalm 35:27
"... Let them say continually, Let the LORD be magnified, which hath pleasure in the prosperity of his servant."
Hebrews 13:15
"By him therefore let us offer the sacrifice of praise to God continually, that is, the fruit of [our] lips giving thanks to his name."
Psalm 34:1
"I WILL bless the LORD at all times: his praise [shall] continually [be] in my mouth."
Psalm 117:1-2
"O PRAISE the LORD, all ye nations: praise him, all ye people. For his merciful kindness is great toward us: and the truth of the LORD [endureth] for ever. Praise ye the LORD."
I Chronicles 29:11
"Thine, O LORD, [is] the greatness, and the power, and the glory, and the victory, and the majesty: for all [that is] in the heaven and in the earth [is thine];

thine [is] the kingdom, O LORD, and thou art exalted as head above all."
I Chronicles 29:12
"Both riches and honour [come] of thee, and thou reignest over all; and in thine hand [is] power and might; and in thine hand [it is] to make great, and to give strength unto all."
I Chronicles 29:13
"Now therefore, our God, we thank thee, and praise thy glorious name."
II Chronicles 20:21
"And when he had consulted with the people, he appointed singers unto the LORD, and that should praise the beauty of holiness, as they went out before the army, and to say, Praise the LORD; for his mercy [endureth] for ever."
II Corinthians 2:14
"Now thanks [be] unto God, which always causeth us to triumph in Christ, and maketh manifest the savour of his knowledge by us in every place."
II Corinthians 4:15
"For all things [are] for your sakes, that the abundant grace might through the thanksgiving of many redound (abound) to the glory of God."
II Corinthians 9:11
"Being enriched in every thing to all bountifulness, which causeth through us thanksgiving to God."
Philippians 3:1
"FINALLY, my brethren, rejoice in the Lord..."
Philippians 4:4
"Rejoice in the Lord alway: [and] again I say, Rejoice."
Philippians 4:6

"Be careful (anxious) for nothing; but in every thing by prayer and supplication with thanksgiving let your requests be made known unto God."

Romans 4:20

"He staggered not at the promise of God through unbelief; but was strong in faith, giving glory to God."

Ephesians 1:6

"To the praise of the glory of his grace, wherein he hath made us accepted in the beloved."

Jude 1:25

"To the only wise God our Saviour, [be] glory and majesty, dominion and power, both now and ever. Amen."

Prayer/Praying in the Spirit

Luke 18:1
"And he spake a parable unto them [to this end], that men ought always to pray, and not to faint."
Luke 19:46
"Saying unto them, It is written, My house is the house of prayer..."
Psalm 4:1
"HEAR me when I call, O God of my righteousness: thou hast enlarged me [when I was] in distress; have mercy upon me, and hear my prayer."
Psalm 5:2
"Hearken unto the voice of my cry, my King, and my God: for unto thee will I pray."
Genesis 25:22
"And the children struggled together within her; and she said, If [it be] so, why [am] I thus? And she went to inquire of the LORD."
Philippians 4:6
"Be careful for nothing; but in every thing by prayer and supplication with thanksgiving let your requests be made know unto God."
I Timothy 2:1-3
"I EXHORT therefore, that, first of all, supplications, prayers, intercessions, [and] giving of thanks, be made for all men: For kings, and [for] all that are in authority; that we may lead a quiet and peaceable life in all godliness and honesty. For this [is] good and acceptable in the sight of God our Saviour."
Colossians 4:2
"Continue in prayer, and watch in the same with thanksgiving."
Philippians 1:4

"Always in every prayer of mine for you all making request with joy."
I Thessalonians 5:17
"Pray without ceasing."
Psalm 102:1-2
"HEAR my prayer, O LORD, and let my cry come unto me. Hide not thy face from me in the day [when] I am in trouble; incline thine ear unto me: in the day [when] I call answer me speedily."
I John 5:14-15
"And this is the confidence that we have in him, that, if we ask any thing according to his will, he heareth us: And if we know that he hear us, whatsoever we ask, we know that we have the petitions that we desired of him."
I Samuel 1:17
".... Go in peace: and the God of Israel grant [thee] thy petition that thou hast asked of him."
Jude 1:20
"But ye, beloved, building up yourselves on your most holy faith, praying in the Holy Ghost."
Ephesians 6:18
"Praying always with all prayer and supplication in the Spirit, and watching thereunto with all perseverance and supplication for all saints."
I Corinthians 14:13,15
"Wherefore let him that speaketh in an [unknown] tongue pray that he may interpret. What is it then? I will pray with the spirit, and I will pray with the understanding also: I will sing with the spirit, and I will sing with the understanding also."
I Corinthians 2:10

"But God hath revealed [them] unto us by his Spirit: for the Spirit searcheth all things, yea, the deep things of God."

Romans 8:26-28

"Likewise the Spirit also helpeth our infirmities: for we know not what we should pray for as we ought: but the Spirit itself maketh intercession for us with groanings which cannot be uttered. And he that searcheth the hearts knoweth what [is] the mind of the Spirit, because he maketh intercession for the saints according to [the will of] God. And we know that all things work together for good to them that love God, to them who are the called according to [his] purpose."

Protection

Exodus 12:13
"And the blood shall be to you for a token upon the houses where ye [are]: and when I see the blood, I will pass over you, and the plague shall not be upon you to destroy [you]…"
I Chronicles 16:20-22
"And [when] they went from nation to nation, and from [one] kingdom to another people; He suffered no man to do them wrong: yea, he reproved kings for their sakes, [Saying] Touch not mine anointed, and do my prophets no harm."
 Isaiah 32:18
"And my people shall dwell in a peaceable habitation, and in sure dwellings, and in quiet resting places."
Psalm 121:8
"The LORD shall preserve thy going out and thy coming in from this time forth, and even for evermore."
Psalm 122:7-8
"Peace be within thy walls, [and] prosperity within thy palaces. For my brethren and companion's sakes, I will now say, Peace [be] within thee."
Psalm 4:8
"I will both lay me down in peace, and sleep: for thou, LORD, only makest me dwell in safety."
Psalm 115:11
"Ye that fear (reverence) the LORD, trust in the LORD: he [is] their help and their shield."
Psalm 12:5

"For the oppression of the poor, for the sighing of the needy, now will I arise, saith the LORD; I will set [him] in safety [from him that] puffeth at him."

Proverbs 21:31

"The horse [is] prepared against the day of battle: but safety [is] of the LORD."

Isaiah 54:17

"No weapon that is formed against thee shall prosper; and every tongue [that] shall rise against thee in judgment thou shalt condemn. This [is] the heritage of the servants of the LORD, and their righteousness [is] of me, saith the LORD."

Zechariah 2:5

"For I, saith the LORD, will be unto her a wall of fire round about, and will be the glory in the midst of her."

Luke 10:19

"Behold, I give you power to tread on serpents and scorpions, and over all the power of the enemy: and nothing shall by any means hurt you."

II Timothy 4:17

"Notwithstanding the Lord stood with me, and strengthened me...and I was delivered out of the mouth of the lion."

II Timothy 4:18

"And the Lord shall deliver me from every evil work, and will preserve [me] unto his heavenly kingdom: to whom [be] glory for ever and ever. Amen."

Job 11:18

"And thou shalt be secure, because there is hope; yea, thou shalt dig [about thee, and] thou shalt take thy rest in safety."

Psalm 91- The Entire Chapter – A few verses

Psalm 91:1

"HE that dwelleth in the secret place of the most High shall abide under the shadow of the Almighty."

Psalm 91:2

"I will say of the LORD, [He is] my refuge and my fortress: my God; in him will I trust."

Psalm 91:10

"There shall no evil befall thee, neither shall any plague come nigh thy dwelling."

Psalm 91:11-12

"For he shall give his angels charge over thee, to keep thee in all thy ways. They shall bear thee up in [their] hands, lest thou dash thy foot against a stone."

Relationships

Proverbs 18:24
"A man [that hath] friends must shew himself friendly: and there is a friend [that] sticketh closer than a brother."
James 2:23
".... Abraham... was called the Friend of God."
III John 1:14
".... [Our] friends salute thee. Greet the friends by name."
Genesis 2:18
"And the LORD God said, [It is] not good that the man should be alone; I will make him an help meet for him."
Ecclesiastes 4:9; 12
"Two [are] better than one; because they have a good reward for their labour. And if one prevail against him, two shall withstand him; and a threefold cord is not quickly broken."
Amos 3:3
"Can two walk together, except they be agreed?"
Romans 12:4-5
"For as we have many members in one body, and all members have not the same office: So we, [being] many, are one body in Christ, and every one members one of another."
Matthew 18:19-20
"Again I say unto you, That if two of you shall agree on earth as touching any thing that they shall ask, it shall be done for them of my Father which is in heaven. For where two or three are gathered together in my name, there am I in the midst of them."

Isaiah 34:16

"Seek ye out of the book of the LORD, and read: no one of these shall fail, none shall want her mate: for my mouth it hath commanded, and his spirit it hath gathered them."

Romans 8:15

"For ye have not received the spirit of bondage again to fear; but ye have received the Spirit of adoption, whereby we cry, Abba, Father."

Isaiah 54:5

"For thy Maker [is] thine husband; the LORD of hosts [is] his name; and thy Redeemer the Holy One of Israel; The God of the whole earth shall he be called."

Romans 1:12

"That is, that I may be comforted together with you by the mutual faith both of you and me."

Philippians 1:3-5

"I thank my God upon every remembrance of you, Always in every prayer of mine for you all making request with joy, For your fellowship in the gospel from the first day until now."

Proverbs 18:22

"[Whoso] findeth a wife findeth a good [thing], and obtaineth favour of the LORD."

John 14:21

"He that hath my commandments, and keepeth them, he it is that loveth me: and he that loveth me shall be loved of my Father, and I will love him, and will manifest myself to him."

Philippians 2:7

"But made himself of no reputation, and took upon him the form of a servant, and was made in the likeness of men."

Ephesians 5:30

"For we are members of his body, of his flesh, and of his bones."

Ephesians 5:31

"For this cause shall a man leave his father and mother, and shall be joined unto his wife, and they two shall be one flesh."

John 13:35

"By this shall all [men] know that ye are my disciples, if ye have love one to another."

Matthew 12:50

"For whosoever shall do the will of my Father which is in heaven, the same is my brother, and sister and mother."

Resurrection

Matthew 17:9
"And as they came down from the mountain, Jesus charged (commanded) them, saying, Tell the vision to no man, until the Son of man be risen again from the dead."

Luke 24:34
"Saying, The Lord is risen indeed, and hath appeared to Simon."

Luke 24:46
"And said unto them, Thus it is written, and thus it behoved Christ to suffer, and rise from the dead the third day."

I Corinthians 15:4-6
"And that he was buried, and that he rose again the third day according to the scriptures: And that he was seen of Cephas, then of the twelve: After that, he was seen of above five hundred brethren at once; of whom the greater part remain unto this present, but some are fallen asleep."

Acts 26:23
"That Christ should suffer, [and] that he should be the first that should rise from the dead, and should shew light unto the people, and to the Gentiles."

Romans 6:4
"Therefore we are buried with him by baptism into death: that like as Christ was raised up from the dead by the glory of the Father, even so we also should walk in newness of life."

Colossians 2:12
"Buried with him in baptism, wherein also ye are risen with [him] through the faith of the operation of God, who hath raised him from the dead."

Romans 8:11

"But if the Spirit of him that raised up Jesus from the dead dwell in you, he that raised up Christ from the dead shall also quicken your mortal bodies by his Spirit that dwelleth in you."

I Thessalonians 4:14

"For if we believe that Jesus died and rose again, even so them also which sleep in Jesus will God bring with him."

Colossians 3:1

"IF ye then be risen with Christ, seek those things which are above, where Christ sitteth on the right hand of God."

Ephesians 1:20

"Which he wrought in Christ, when he raised him from the dead, and set [him] at his own right hand in the heavenly [places]."

Ephesians 2:6

"And hath raised [us] up together, and made [us] sit together in heavenly [places] in Christ Jesus."

II Corinthians 5:15

"And [that] he died for all, that they which live should not henceforth live unto themselves, but unto him which died for them, and rose again."

Acts 17:28

"For in him we live, and move, and have our being..."

Romans 8:34

"Who [is] he that condemneth? [It is] Christ that died, yea rather, that is risen again, who is even at the right hand of God, who also maketh intercession for us."

Galatians 2:20

"I am crucified with Christ: nevertheless I live; yet not I, but Christ liveth in me: and the life which I now live in the flesh I live by the faith of the Son of God, who loved me, and gave himself for me."

Righteousness

Genesis 15:6
"And he (Abraham) believed in the LORD; and he (God) counted it to him for righteousness."

Romans 4:3; 13
"For what saith the scripture? Abraham believed God, and it was counted unto him for righteousness. For the promise, that he should be heir of the world, [was] not to Abraham, or to his seed, through the law, but through the righteousness of faith."

Romans 8:10
"And if Christ [be] in you, the body [is] dead because of sin; but the Spirit [is] life because of righteousness."

I Corinthians 1:30
"But of him are ye in Christ Jesus, who of God is made unto us wisdom, and righteousness, and sanctification, and redemption."

II Corinthians 5:21
"For he (God) hath made him (Jesus) [to be] sin for us, who (Jesus) knew no sin; that we might be made the righteousness of God in him."

Galatians 3:6
"Even as Abraham believed God, and it was accounted to him for righteousness."

Isaiah 32:17
"And the work of righteousness shall be peace; and effect of righteousness quietness and assurance for ever."

Romans 3:21-22
"But now the righteousness of God without the law is manifested, being witnessed by the law and the

prophets; Even the righteousness of God [which is] by faith of Jesus Christ unto all and upon all them that believe: for there is no difference."

James 2:23

"And the scripture was fulfilled which saith, Abraham believed God, and it was imputed unto him for righteousness: and he was called the Friend of God."

James 5:16

"...The effectual fervent prayer of a righteous man availeth much."

Proverbs 28:1

"...But the righteous are bold as a lion."

Isaiah 54:14

"In righteousness shalt thou be established: thou shalt be far from oppression; for thou shalt not fear: and from terror; for it shall not come near thee."

Psalm 34:15

"The eyes of the LORD [are] upon the righteous, and his ears [are open] unto their cry."

I Peter 3:12

"For the eyes of the Lord [are] over the righteous, and his ears [are open] unto their prayers..."

I Peter 2:24

"Who his own self bare our sins in his own body on the tree, that we, being dead to sins, should live unto righteousness: by whose stripes ye were healed."

Titus 3:5-7

"Not by works of righteousness which we have done, but according to his mercy he saved us, by the washing of regeneration, and renewing of the Holy Ghost; Which he shed (pored out) on us abundantly through Jesus Christ our Saviour; That being justified by his grace, we should be made heirs according to the hope of eternal life."

Salvation

I Timothy 2:4-6
"Who will have all men to be saved, and to come into the knowledge of the truth. For [there is] one God, and one mediator between God and men, the man Christ Jesus; Who gave himself a ransom for all, to be testified in due time."

John 1:12
"But as many as received him, to them gave he power to become the sons of God, [even] to them that believe on his name."

John 3:3-5
"Jesus answered and said unto him, Verily, verily, I say unto thee, Except a man be born again, he cannot see the kingdom of God. Nicodemus saith unto him, How can a man be born when he is old? can he enter the second time into his mother's womb, and be born? Jesus answered, Verily, verily, I say unto thee, Except a man be born of water and [of] the Spirit, he cannot enter into the kingdom of God."

Romans 10:9-10
"That if thou shalt confess with thy mouth the Lord Jesus, and shalt believe in thine heart that God hath raised him from the dead, thou shalt be saved. For with the heart man believeth unto righteousness; and with the mouth confession is made unto salvation."

Mark 16:16
"He that believeth and is baptized shall be saved; but he that believeth not shall be damned."

Acts 2:38

"Then Peter said unto them, Repent, and be baptized every one of you in the name of Jesus Christ for the remission of sins, and ye shall receive the gift of the Holy Ghost."

Acts 4:12

"Neither is there salvation in any other: for there is none other name under heaven given among men, whereby we must be saved."

Acts 8:36-37

"...And the eunuch said, See, [here is] water; what doth hinder me to be baptized? And Phillip said, If thou believest with all thine heart, thou mayest. And he answered and said, I believe that Jesus Christ is the Son of God."

Acts 16:30-31

".... Sirs, what must I do to be saved? And they said, Believe on the Lord Jesus Christ, and thou shalt be saved, and thy house."

Acts 26:18

"To open their eyes, [and] to turn [them] from darkness to light, and [from] the power of Satan unto God, that they may receive forgiveness of sins, and inheritance among them which are sanctified by faith that is in me."

Philippians 2:9-11

"Wherefore God also hath highly exalted him, and given him a name which is above every name: That at the name of Jesus every knee should bow, of [things] in heaven, and [things] in earth, and [things] under the earth; And [that] every tongue should confess that Jesus Christ [is] Lord, to the glory of God the Father."

Galatians 3:26-27

"For ye are all the children of God by faith in Christ Jesus. For as many of you as have been baptized into Christ have put on Christ."

Sleep/Rest

Job 11:19
"Also thou shalt lie down, and none shall make [thee] afraid...."

Psalm 127:2
"[It is] vain for you to rise up early, to sit up late, to eat the bread of sorrows: [for] so he giveth his beloved sleep."

Psalm 3:5
"I laid me down and slept; I awaked; for the LORD sustained me."

Psalm 4:8
"I will both lay me down in peace, and sleep: for thou, LORD, only makest me dwell in safety."

Proverbs 3:24
"When thou liest down, thou shalt not be afraid: yea, thou shall lie down, and thy sleep shall be sweet."

Proverbs 6:22
"When thou goest, it shall lead thee; when thou sleepest, it shall keep thee; and [when] thou awakest, it shall talk with thee."

John 11:12
"Then said his disciples, Lord, if he sleeps, he shall do well."

Isaiah 32:18
"And my people shall dwell in a peaceable habitation, and in sure dwellings, and in quiet resting places."

Isaiah 30:15
"For thus saith the LORD GOD, the Holy One of Israel; In returning and rest shall ye be saved; in

quietness and in confidence shall be your strength…"
Psalm 116:7
"Return unto thy rest, O my soul; for the LORD hath dealt bountifully with thee."
Psalm 121:3
"He will not suffer thy foot to be moved: he that keepeth thee will not slumber."
Isaiah 14:3
"And it shall come to pass in the day that the LORD shall give thee rest from thy sorrow, and from thy fear, and from the hard bondage wherein thou wast made to serve."
Matthew 11:28-30
"Come unto me, all [ye] that labour and are heavy laden, and I will give you rest. Take my yoke upon you, and learn of me; for I am meek and lowly in heart: and ye shall find rest unto your souls. For my yoke [is] easy, and my burden is light."
Jeremiah 30:10
"…And shall be in rest, and be quiet, and none shall make [him] afraid."
Isaiah 28:12
"To whom he said, This [is] the rest [wherewith] ye may cause the weary to rest; and this [is] the refreshing…"
Acts 2:26
"Therefore did my heart rejoice, and my tongue was glad; moreover also my flesh shall rest in hope."
Proverbs 14:33
"Wisdom resteth in the heart of him that hath understanding…"
Ecclesiastes 5:12

"The sleep of a labouring man [is] sweet…"
<u>Isaiah 63:14</u>
"…The Spirit of the LORD caused him to rest: so didst thou lead thy people, to make thyself a glorious name."
<u>Zephaniah 3:17</u>
"The LORD thy God in the midst of thee [is] mighty; he will save, he will rejoice over thee with joy; he will rest in his love, he will joy over thee with singing."

The Blessing

Genesis 1:28
"And God blessed them, and God said unto them,
Be fruitful, and multiply, and replenish the earth,
and subdue it: and have dominion over the fish of
the sea, and over the fowl of the air, and over
every living thing that moveth upon the earth."
Genesis 9:1; 9
"And God blessed Noah and his sons, and said unto
them, Be fruitful, and multiply, and replenish the
earth. And I, behold, I establish my covenant with
you, and with your seed (descendants) after you."
Genesis 12:2-3
"And I will make of thee a great nation, and I will
bless thee, and make thy name great; and thou
shalt be a blessing: And I will bless them that bless
thee, and curse him that curseth thee: and in thee
shall all families of the earth be blessed."
Genesis 14:19-20
"And he blessed him, and said, Blessed [be] Abram
of the most high God, possessor of heaven and
earth: And blessed be the most high God, which
hath delivered thine enemies into thy hand. And he
gave him tithes of all."
Genesis 18:18
"Seeing that Abraham shall surely become a great
and mighty nation, and all the nations of the earth
shall be blessed in him?"
Genesis 24:1; 31; 60
"And Abraham was old, [and] well stricken in age:
and the LORD had blessed Abraham in all things.
And he said, Come in, thou blessed of the LORD...
And they blessed Rebekah, and said unto her, Thou

[art] our sister, be thou [the mother] of thousands of millions, and let thy seed possess the gate of those which hate them."

Genesis 26:12-13; 29

"Then Isaac sowed in that land, and received (reaped) in the same year and hundredfold: and the LORD blessed him. And the man waxed great, and went forward, and grew until he became very great...Thou [art] now the blessed of the LORD."

Genesis 39:5; 21

"And it came to pass from the time [that] he had made him overseer in his house, and over all that he had, that the LORD blessed the Egyptian's house for Joseph's sake; and the blessing of the LORD was upon all that he had in the house, and in the field. But the LORD was with Joseph, and shewed him mercy, and gave him favour in the sight of the keeper of the prison."

Deuteronomy 7:13

"And he will love thee, and bless thee, and multiply thee: he will also bless the fruit of thy womb, and fruit of thy land, thy corn, and thy wine, and thine oil, the increase of thy kine, and the flocks of thy sheep, in the land which he sware unto thy fathers to give thee."

Psalm 37:22

"For [such as be] blessed of him shall inherit the earth; and [they that be] cursed of him shall be cut off."

Psalm 112:1-3

"PRAISE ye the LORD. Blessed [is] the man [that] feareth (honors) the LORD, [that] delighteth greatly in his commandments. His seed shall be mighty upon earth: the generation of the upright shall be

blessed. Wealth and riches [shall be] in his house: and his righteousness endureth for ever."
Psalm 115:12
"The LORD hath been mindful of us: he will bless [us]; he will bless the house of Israel; he will bless the house of Aaron."
Psalm 115:13
"He will bless them that fear (honor) the LORD, [both] small and great."
Psalm 115:14-15
"The LORD shall increase you more and more, you and your children. Ye [are] blessed of the LORD which made heaven and earth."
Joshua 1:8
"This book of the law shall not depart out of thy mouth; but thou shalt mediate therein day and night, that thou mayest observe to do according to all that is written therein: for then thou shalt make thy way prosperous, and then thou shalt have good success."
Joshua 1:9
"Have not I commanded thee? Be strong and of a good courage; be not afraid, neither be thou dismayed: for the LORD thy God [is] with thee whithersoever thou goest."
Proverbs 10:22
"The blessing of the LORD, it maketh rich, and he addeth no sorrow with it."
Isaiah 65:23
"They shall not labour in vain, nor bring forth for trouble; for they [are] the seed of the blessed of the LORD, and their offspring with them."
Acts 3:25-26

"Ye are the children of the prophets, and of the covenant which God made with our fathers, saying unto Abraham, And in thy seed shall all the kindreds of the earth be blessed. Unto you first God, having raised up his Son Jesus, sent him to bless you, in turning away every one of you from his iniquity."
Acts 10:34-35
"...Of a truth I perceive that God is no respecter of persons: But in every nation he that feareth (respects) him, and worketh righteousness, is accepted with him."
Acts 10:38
"How God anointed Jesus of Nazareth with the Holy Ghost and with power: who went about doing good, and healing all that were oppressed of the devil; for God was with him."
Galatians 3:13-14
"Christ hath redeemed us from the curse of the law, being made a curse for us: for it is written, Cursed [is] every one that hangeth on a tree: That the blessing of Abraham might come on the Gentiles through Jesus Christ; that we might receive the promise of the Spirit through faith."
Galatians 3:26; 29
"For ye are all the children of God by faith in Christ Jesus. And if ye [be] Christ's, then are ye Abraham's seed, and heirs according to the promise."
II Corinthians 8:9
"For you know the grace of our Lord Jesus Christ, that, though he was rich, yet for your sakes he became poor, that ye through his poverty might be rich."
Ephesians 1:3

"Blessed [be] the God and Father of our Lord Jesus Christ, who hath blessed us with all spiritual blessings in heavenly [places] in Christ."

III John 1:2

"Beloved, I wish above all things that thou mayest prosper and be in health, even as thy soul prospereth."

Isaiah 48:17

"...I [am] the LORD thy God which teacheth thee to profit, which leadeth thee by the way [that] thou shouldest go."

Philippians 4:19

"But my God shall supply all your need according to his riches in glory by Christ Jesus."

II Corinthians 9:8

"And God [is] able to make all grace abound toward you; that ye, always having all sufficiency in all [things], may abound to every good work."

Psalm 113:7-8

"He raiseth up the poor out of the dust, [and] lifteth the needy out of the dunghill; That he may set [him] with princes, [even] with the princes of his people."

The Holy Spirit

Joel 2:28-29

"And it shall come to pass afterward, [that] I will pour out my spirit upon all flesh; and your sons and your daughters shall prophecy, your old men shall dream dreams, your young men shall see visions: And also upon the servants and upon the handmaids in those days will I pour out my spirit."

John 1:33

"...But he that sent me to baptize with water, the same said unto me, Upon whom thou shalt see the Spirit descending, and remaining on him, the same is he which baptizeth with the Holy Ghost."

Acts 1:4-5

"And, being assembled together with [them], commanded them that they should not depart from Jerusalem, but wait for the promise of the Father, which, [saith he], ye have heard of me. For John truly baptized with water; but ye shall be baptized with the Holy Ghost not many days hence."

John 14:16-17

"And I will pray the Father, and he shall give you another Comforter, that he may abide with you for ever; [Even] the Spirit of truth; whom the world cannot receive, because it seeth him not, neither knoweth him: but ye know him; for he dwelleth with you, and shall be in you."

John 14:26

"But the Comforter, [which is] the Holy Ghost, whom the Father will send in my name, he shall teach you all things, and bring all things to your remembrance, whatsoever I have said unto you."

John 16:13-14

"Howbeit when he, the Spirit of truth, is come, he will guide you into all truth: for he shall not speak of himself; but whatsoever he shall hear, [that] shall he speak: and he will shew you things to come. He shall glorify me: for he shall receive of mine, and shall shew [it] unto you."

Acts 6:3

"Wherefore, brethren, look ye out among you seven men of honest report, full of the Holy Ghost and wisdom, whom we may appoint over this business."

Romans 8:26-28

"Likewise the Spirit also helpeth our infirmities (weaknesses): for we know not what we should pray for as we ought: but the Spirit itself maketh intercession for us with groanings which cannot be uttered. And he that searcheth the hearts knoweth what [is] the mind of the Spirit, because he maketh intercession for the saints according to [the will of] God. And we know that all things work together for good to them that love God, to them who are the called according to [his] purpose."

I Corinthians 2:9-10

"But as it is written, Eye hath not seen, nor ear heard, neither have entered into the heart of man, the things which God hath prepared for them that love him. But God hath revealed [them] unto us by his Spirit: for the Spirit searcheth all things, yea, the deep things of God."

I Corinthians 2:13-16

"Which things also we speak, not in the words which man's wisdom teacheth, but which the Holy Ghost teacheth; comparing spiritual things with spiritual. But the natural man receiveth not the things of the Spirit of God: for they are foolishness unto him: neither can he know [them], because they are spiritually discerned. But he that is spiritual judgeth all things, yet he himself is judged of no man. For who hath known the mind of the Lord, that he may instruct him? But we have the mind of Christ."

The Name of Jesus

Proverbs 18:10
"The name of the LORD [is] a strong tower: the righteous runneth into it, and is safe."
Matthew 18:5
"And whoso shall receive one such little child in my name receiveth me."
Matthew 18:20
"For where two or three are gathered together in my name, there am I in the midst of them."
Mark 16:17-18
"And these signs shall follow them that believe; In my name shall they cast out devils; they shall speak with new tongues; They shall take up serpents; and if they drink any deadly thing, it shall not hurt them; they shall lay hands on the sick, and they shall recover."
Philippians 2:10
"That at the name of Jesus every knee should bow, of [things] in heaven and [things] in earth, and [things] under the earth."
Romans 14:11
"For it is written, [As] I live, saith the Lord, every knee shall bow to me, and every tongue shall confess to God."
John 16:23
"And in that day ye shall ask me nothing. Verily, verily, I say unto you, Whatsoever ye shall ask the Father in my name, he will give [it] you."
John 14:13-14
"And whatsoever ye shall ask in my name, that will I do, that the Father may be glorified in the Son. If ye shall ask any thing in my name, I will do [it]."

John 14:26

"But the Comforter, [which is] the Holy Ghost, whom the Father will send in my name, he shall teach you all things, and bring all things to your remembrance, whatsoever I have said unto you."

John 15:16

"Ye have not chosen me, but I have chosen you, and ordained you, that ye should go and bring forth fruit, and [that] your fruit should remain: that whatsoever ye shall ask of the Father in my name, he may give it you."

Acts 9:15

"But the Lord said unto him, Go thy way: for he is a chosen vessel unto me, to bear my name before the Gentiles, and kings, and the children of Israel."

Acts 3:16

"And his name through faith in his name hath made this man strong, whom ye see and know: yea, the faith which is by him hath given him this perfect soundness in the presence of you all."

Acts 4:10

"Be it known unto you all, and to all the people of Israel, that by the name of Jesus Christ of Nazareth, whom ye crucified, whom God raised from the dead, [even] by him doth this man stand here before you whole."

Acts 4:30

"By stretching forth thine hand to heal; and that signs and wonders may be done by the name of thy holy child Jesus."

Acts 28:31

"Preaching the kingdom of God, and teaching those things which concern the Lord Jesus Christ, with all confidence, no man forbidding him."

I John 3:23

"And this is his commandment, That we should believe on the name of his Son Jesus Christ, and love one another, as he gave us commandment."

I John 5:13

"These things have I written unto you that believe on the name of the Son of God; that ye may know that ye have eternal life, and that ye may believe on the name of the Son of God."

Ephesians 1:20-23

"Which he wrought in Christ, when he raised him from the dead, and set [him] at his own right hand in the heavenly [places], Far above all principality, and power, and might, and dominion, and every name that is named, not only in this world, but also in that which is to come: And hath put all [things] under his feet, and gave him [to be] the head over all [things] to the church, Which is his body, the fullness of him that filleth all in all."

Colossians 1:12-13

"Giving thanks unto the Father, which hath made us meet (able) to be partakers of the inheritance of the saints in light: Who hath delivered us from the power of darkness, and hath translated [us] into the kingdom of his dear Son."

Colossians 1:14-15

"In whom we have redemption through his blood, [even] the forgiveness of sins: Who is the image of the invisible God, the firstborn of every creature."

Colossians 1:16-17

"For by him were all things created, that are in heaven, and that are in earth, visible and invisible, whether [they be] thrones, or dominions, or principalities, or powers: all things were created by

him, and for him: And he is before all things, and
be him all things consist."

Colossians 1:18

"And he is the head of the body, the church: who is
the beginning, the firstborn from the dead; that in
all [things] he might have the preeminence."

Colossians 3:17

"And whatsoever ye do in word or deed, [do] all in
the name of the Lord Jesus, giving thanks to God
and the Father by him."

Psalm 89:24

"But my faithfulness and my mercy [shall be] with
him: and in my name shall his horn be exalted."

Revelation 2:13

"...And thou holdest fast my name, and hast not
denied my faith..."

The Word of God

Proverbs 4:20-22
"My son, attend to my words; incline thine ear unto my sayings. Let them not depart from thine eyes; keep them in the midst of thine heart. For they [are] life unto those that find them, and health to all their flesh."

Matthew 4:4
"But he (Jesus) answered and said, It is written, Man shall not live by bread alone, but by every word that proceedeth out of the mouth of God."

Psalm 89:34
"My covenant will I not break, nor alter the thing that is gone out of my lips."

Numbers 23:19
"God [is] not a man, that he should lie; neither the son of man, that he should repent: hath he said, and shall he not do [it]? or hath he spoken, and shall he not make it good?"

Genesis 21:1
"And the LORD visited Sarah as he had said, and the LORD did unto Sarah as he had spoken."

I Kings 8:56
"Blessed [be] the LORD, that hath given rest unto his people Israel, according to all that he promised: there hath not failed one word of all his good promise, which he promised by the hand of Moses his servant."

John 6:63
"It is the spirit that quickeneth (makes alive); the flesh profiteth nothing: the words that I speak unto, [they] are spirit, and [they] are life."

Isaiah 55:11

"So shall my word be that goeth forth out of my mouth: it shall not return unto me void, but it shall accomplish that which I please, and prosper [in the thing] whereto I send it."

Hebrews 1:3

"...And upholding all things by the word of his power..."

Psalm 33:6

"By the word of the LORD were the heavens made; and all the host of them by the breath of his mouth."

Hebrews 4:12

"For the word of God [is] quick, and powerful, and sharper than any twoedged sword, piercing even to the dividing asunder of soul and spirit, and of the joints and marrow, and [is] a discerner of the thoughts and intents of the heart."

Jeremiah 15:16

"Thy words were found, and I did eat them, and thy word was unto me the joy and rejoicing of mine heart: for I am called by thy name, O LORD God of hosts."

Psalm 103:20

"Bless the LORD, ye his angels, that excel in strength, that do his commandments, hearkening unto the voice of his word."

Deuteronomy 11:19

"And ye shall teach them your children, speaking of them when thou sittest in thine house, and when thou walkest by the way, when thou liest down, and when thou risest up."

Colossians 3:16

"Let the word of Christ dwell in you richly in all wisdom; teaching and admonishing one another in psalms and hymns and spiritual songs, singing with grace in your hearts to the Lord."

John 14:10; 12

"Believest thou not that I am in the Father, and the Father in me? the words that I speak unto you I speak not of myself: but the Father that dwelleth in me, he doeth the works. Verily, verily, I say unto you, He that believeth on me, the works that I do shall he do also; and greater [works] than these shall he do; because I go unto my Father."

Psalm 119 the Entire Chapter – A few verses

Psalm 119:11

"Thy word have I hid in mine heart, that I might not sin against thee."

Psalm 119:16

"I will delight myself in thy statutes: I will not forget thy word."

Psalm 119:28

"My soul melteth for heaviness: strengthen thou me according unto thy word."

Psalm 119:105

"Thy word [is] a lamp unto my feet, and a light unto my path."

Wisdom

James 1:5-8
"If any of you lack wisdom, let him ask of God, that giveth to all [men] liberally, and upbraideth not; and it shall be given him. But let him ask in faith, nothing wavering. For he that wavereth is like a wave of the sea driven with the wind and tossed. For let not that man think that he shall receive any thing of the Lord. A double minded man [is] unstable in all his ways."

Isaiah 33:6
"And wisdom and knowledge shall be the stability of thy times, [and] strength of salvation: the fear (reverence) of the LORD is his treasure."

Ecclesiastes 7:11
"Wisdom [is] good with an inheritance: and [by it there is] profit to them that see the sun."

Ecclesiastes 7:12
"For wisdom [is] a defence, [and] money [is] a defence: but the excellency of knowledge [is, that] wisdom giveth life to them that have it."

Daniel 1:20
"And in all matters of wisdom [and] understanding, that the king enquired of them, he found them ten times better than all the magicians [and] astrologers that [were] in all his realm."

I Corinthians 1:30-31
"But of him are ye in Christ Jesus, who of God is made unto us wisdom, and righteousness, and sanctification, and redemption: That, according as it is written, He that glorieth, let him glory in the Lord."

Genesis 41:16; 39; 41

"And Joseph answered Pharaoh, saying, [It is] not in me: God shall give Pharaoh an answer of peace. And Pharaoh said unto Joseph, Forasmuch as God hath shewed thee all this, [there is] none so discreet and wise as thou [art]: And Pharaoh said unto Joseph, See, I have set thee over all the land of Egypt."

Isaiah 50:4-5

"The LORD GOD hath given me the tongue of the learned, that I should know how to speak a word in season to [him that is] weary: he wakeneth morning by morning, he wakeneth mine ear to hear as the learned. The Lord GOD hath opened mine ear, and I was not rebellious, neither turned away back."

Jeremiah 33:3

"Call unto me, and I will answer thee, and shew thee great and mighty things, which thou knowest not."

Isaiah 52:13

"Behold, my servant shall deal prudently, he shall be exalted and extolled, and be very high."

James 3:13

"Who [is] a wise man and endured with knowledge among you? let him shew out of a good conversation his works with meekness of wisdom."

James 3:17

"But the wisdom that is from above is first pure, then peaceable, gentle, [and] easy to be intreated, full of mercy and good fruits, without partiality, and without hypocrisy."

Colossians 2:3

"In whom are hid all the treasures of wisdom and knowledge."

I Corinthians 2:4

"And my speech and my preaching [was] not with enticing words of man's wisdom, but in demonstration of the Spirit and of power."

I Corinthians 2:5

"That your faith should not stand in the wisdom of men, but in the power of God."

Exodus 35:31

"And he hath filled him with the spirit of God, in wisdom, in understanding, and in knowledge, and in all manner of workmanship."

Luke 21:15

"For I will give you a mouth and wisdom, which all your adversaries shall not be able to gainsay (refute) nor resist."

Acts 6:10

"And they were not able to resist the wisdom and the spirit by which he spake."

Exodus 4:12

"Now therefore go, and I will be with thy mouth, and teach thee what thou shalt say."

THE ENTIRE BOOK OF PROVERBS- A few examples

Proverbs 4:7

"Wisdom [is] the principal thing; [therefore] get wisdom: and with all thy getting get understanding."

Proverbs 5:1-2

"MY son, attend unto my wisdom, [and] bow thine ear to my understanding: That thou mayest regard discretion, and [that] thy lips may keep knowledge."

Proverbs 1:20

"Wisdom crieth without; she uttereth her voice in the streets."

Proverbs 2:6-7

"For the LORD giveth wisdom: out of his mouth [cometh] knowledge and understanding. He layeth up sound wisdom for the righteous: [he is] a buckler to them that walk uprightly."

Proverbs 2:10-11

"When wisdom entereth into thine heart, and knowledge is pleasant to thy soul. Discretion shall preserve thee, understanding shall keep thee."

Proverbs 3:13; 16

"Happy [is] the man [that] findeth wisdom, and the man [that] getteth understanding. Length of days [is] in her right hand; [and] in her left hand riches and honour."

Proverbs 14:1

"EVERY wise woman buildeth her house: but the foolish plucketh it down with her hands."

Proverbs 19:8

"He that getteth wisdom loveth his own soul: he that keepeth understanding shall find good."

Proverbs 19:20

"Hear counsel, and receive instruction, that thou mayest be wise in thy latter end."

Proverbs 24:3-5

"Through wisdom is an house builded; and by understanding it is established: And by knowledge shall the chambers be filled with all precious and pleasant riches. A wise man [is] strong; yea, a man of knowledge increaseth strength."

KCM Resources

Kenneth Copland Ministries

Fort Worth, TX 76192-0001
www.kcm.org
1-800-600-7395

Prayer line 24 hours every day in the
United States 1-817-852-6000
For contact information outside of the US- write
or call United States Ministry Office

Free Believer's Voice of Victory Magazine
Call 1-800-600-7395 or KCM.ORG/MAG

Kenneth Copland Ministries offers a free
Salvation Package in English and other languages.
The website has prayers and resources that can be
printed free. Also, there is a daily on line free
devotional "Faith to Faith."

At the KCM online store there are resources that
I found extremely helpful in my recovery and daily
life. There are six LifeLine Kits that are 10-day
Spiritual Action Plans that can be purchased for
comprehensive step-by step instructions and help.
The topics are: **Healing**, **Financial Breakthrough**,
Relationships, **Answered Prayers**, **Faith that Can
Move Mountains** and new in 2015 **Overcoming
Stress, Anxiety & Depression.** Each LifeLine Kit
includes a quick-start guide, an interactive
devotional book, and scriptures readings on CD,
worship music, DVD teaching and take along faith-
in-action cards.

Prayer from the KCM website

**These are not exact quotes from the Bible.
These are paraphrased scriptures.**

A CONFESSION OF VICTORY OVER DEFEAT

Thank You Lord that the devil is a powerless, defeated foe! And, in Christ Jesus I am victorious! I am not moved by overwhelming feelings or past failures because God is bigger and more powerful than anything and everything I've ever been through. I walk in the promises God has for me and my mind is transformed by His Word.

I command all strongholds to bend their knee to the authority of Jesus Christ! No matter what my situation looks like, I choose to believe God's truth and tear down the devil's lies. I am not defeated! I have set my hope in Jesus and by faith I walk in victory!

Confession References (Colossians 2:13-15, I Corinthians 15:57, I John 4:4, Romans 12:2, II Corinthians 10:3-5, II Corinthians 1:10-11, I John 5:4)

PRAYER OF SALVATION AND BAPTISM IN THE HOLY SPIRIT

(THIS IS FROM THE KCM WEBSITE)

If you do not know Jesus as your Savior and Lord, simply pray the following prayer in faith, and Jesus will be your Lord!

"Heavenly Father, I come to You in the Name of Jesus. Your Word says, 'Whosoever shall call on the name of the Lord shall be saved' (**Acts 2:21**). I am calling on You. I pray and ask Jesus to come into my heart and be Lord over my life according to **Romans 10:9-10**: 'If thou shalt confess with thy mouth the Lord Jesus, and shalt believe in thine heart that God has raised him from the dead, thou shalt be saved. For with the heart man believeth unto righteousness; and with the mouth confession is made unto salvation.' I do that now. I confess that Jesus is Lord, and I believe in my heart that God raised Him from the dead.
"I am now reborn! I am a Christian—a child of Almighty God! I am saved! You also said in Your Word, 'If ye then being evil, know how to give good gifts unto your children: HOW MUCH MORE shall your heavenly Father give the Holy Spirit to them that ask him?' (**Luke 11:13**). I'm also asking You to fill me with the Holy Spirit. Holy Spirit, rise up within me as I praise God. I fully expect to speak with other tongues as You give me the utterance (**Acts 2:4**). In Jesus' Name. Amen!"

Begin to praise God for filling you with the Holy Spirit. Speak those words and syllables you receive—not in your own language, but the language given to you by the Holy Spirit. You have to use your own voice. God will not force you to speak. Don't be concerned with how it sounds. It is a heavenly language!

Continue with the blessing God has given you and pray in tongues each day. You are a born-again, Spirit-filled believer. You'll never be the same!

If you have just prayed this prayer, please contact us and let us know of your decision. We have a free Salvation Package we would like to send you to help you begin your new life in Jesus!

Learn More About Your Salvation

If you have prayed this prayer, welcome to the family of God. We would like to send you some materials that will help you to get started on your new walk with the Lord!

Go to www.kcm.org to receive a free Salvation Package, today.

Your Salvation Package will be shipped to you free of charge and will include the book *He Did It All for You* (a compilation of the mini books *Welcome to the Family, Love-The Secret to Your Success, The Force of Righteousness, Now Are We In Christ Jesus* and *God's Will Is the Holy Spirit*) and the *How to Study the Bible* brochure by Kenneth Copeland.

Made in the USA
Middletown, DE
20 November 2015